alfabet / alphabet

alfabet / alphabet

a memoir of a first language

Sadiqa de Meijer

Palimpsest Press
1171 Eastlawn Ave.
Windsor, Ontario. N8S 3J1
www.palimpsestpress.ca

Printed and bound in Canada
Cover design and book typography by Ellie Hastings
Edited by Jim Johnstone
Cover Photograph by C.A. Smid

Palimpsest Press would like to thank the Canada Council for the Arts and
the Ontario Arts Council for their support of our publishing program.
We also acknowledge the assistance of the Government of Ontario
through the Ontario Book Publishing Tax Credit.

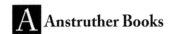

A Anstruther Books

LIBRARY AND ARCHIVES CANADA CATALOGUING IN PUBLICATION

TITLE: Alfabet / alphabet : a memoir of a first language / Sadiqa de Meijer.
NAMES: De Meijer, Sadiqa, 1977- author.
IDENTIFIERS: Canadiana (print) 20200277227
Canadiana (ebook) 20200277596

ISBN 9781989287606 (softcover) | ISBN 9781989287613 (EPUB)
ISBN 9781989287620 (Kindle) | ISBN 9781989287637 (PDF)

SUBJECTS: LCSH: De Meijer, Sadiqa, 1977-
LCSH: Second language acquisition—Anecdotes.
LCSH: English language—Acquisition—Anecdotes.
CSH: Second language learners' writings, Canadian (English)
LCGFT: Autobiographies.

CLASSIFICATION: LCC PS8607.E4822 Z46 2020 | DDC C818/.603—dc23

For each of you who came to English from some beloved elsewhere.

De taal is ons vaderland, waaruit we nooit kunnen emigreren.

Language is our fatherland, from which we can never emigrate.

—Irina Grivnina

accent / accent

My mother's vowels were clear as drinking water. She expected ours to sound the same.

She was a teacher, and the child of two teachers; before them, there was a madwoman, a sea captain, a divorcée, a drunk. And then blacksmiths, generations of them, clanging out horseshoes on inherited anvils.

"The finest Dutch," she used to say, "is spoken in Haarlem." That wasn't where we lived.

I thought of the song about the bells.

The clocks of Haarlem, they sound sweet of tone.

The Dutch words for sound (the verb) and vowel are very close: *klinken* and *klinker*. The bricks of the old streets are also called *klinkers*, which has to do with the archaic term *inklinken*, to shrink down or dry or compress a material.

When I was in first grade, our class visited an abandoned brick factory on the Rijn.

We knew the ruined structure as the backdrop to a quarry. People swam there in the summers. Our cupped hands, plunged in the shallows, would emerge crowded with wriggling tadpoles. *Dikkopjes*; little fat heads.

The building that had manufactured bricks was also made of bricks: one tall, round chimney, a row of arched ovens with crumbling walls, and a roof overgrown with dandelions. Our guide had worked at the factory. The river clay, he explained, had been dug from where the quarry now was, then purified and shaped and baked. He told us the quality of bricks can be confirmed by listening for their lucid, musical pitch when banged together.

We were from schoolteachers, and we would sound like it.

Not from market vendors, who spoke the Dutch of our region: grammatically pragmatic, lower in pitch, with languidly melodic tones. That was called flat—it had to do, a long time ago, with the elevations of the land.

And also not from the Queen, with her architectural hats, her bruised and reticent inflections. That was talking with a hot potato in your mouth.

What a tough and lovely feeling it was to slip into the vernacular on the streets. To skin a knee and pronounce "I'm bleeding" as "I bloom."

Mother tongue; in her book on the subject, Yasemin Yildiz warns us against the term's implied assumption that a first language carries an "affective and corporeal intimacy."

Oh, but Dutch is indeed my mother tongue.

My pulse music, my bone resonator, my umbilical ligature.

"The milk language," says Ghita El Khayat, who published *Le Petit Prince* in its first dialectical Arabic translation, "because such a story is a gift from mother to child."

My language of lullaby and nursery rhyme.

My language of the effortless diminutive, the suffix *je*, which, in the vocabulary of early childhood, when doorways and hedges and grown-ups towered over us, seemed to permeate our portion of the world:

dutje, kusje, laarsje, kindje   nap, kiss, boot, child

And when I stood on the low plaster toadstool that served as a trail marker in the woods near Ede, still too small to get there without someone lifting me or to leap off without clutching their hand, it was the language of first namings: *boom, grond, lucht*. Are there any spoken sounds as elemental? Not to the anvil bone of my inner ear.

Boom, grond and *lucht* exist where I live now, as well: trees, ground, and sky.

The ground is not that old ground; it is another continent.

The sky is continuous with the old one, but it feels different. It isn't as vast and fresh, or as haunted by hurried clouds. Here the people do not call it *lucht,* and so it isn't also air, which means it is impossible to breathe this sky.

Sky cannot fill your lungs or flow into your bloodstream.

Only *lucht* can do that.

bitter / bitter

Boutade

O land van mist en mest, van vuile, koude regen,
Doorsijperd stukje grond, vol kille dauw en damp,
Vol vuns, onpeilbaar slijk en ondoorwaadbare wegen,
Vol jicht en paraplu's, vol kiespijn en vol kramp!

O saaie brij-moeras, o erf van overschoenen,
Van kikkers, baggerlui, schoenlappers, moddergoden,
Van eenden groot en klein, in allerlei fatsoenen,
Ontvang het najaarswee van uw verkouden zoon!

Uw kliemerig klimaat maakt mij het bloed in de
aderen
tot modder: 'k heb geen lied, geen honger, vreugd
noch vree.
Trek overschoenen aan, gewijde grond der Vaderen,
Gij - niet op mijn verzoek - ontwoekerd aan de zee.

P.A. de Genestet (1829-1861)

Boutade

O land of manure and mist, of cold and foul rain,
Small sodden ground, full of frigid dew and damp,
Of fens, fathomless mud and flooded lanes,
Of gout and umbrellas, toothaches and cramp!

O boring porridge-swamp, o yard of overshoes,
Of frogs, dredgers, cobblers, gods of clay,
Of ducks large and small, in every hue,
Receive your coughing son's autumn dismay!

Your dank climate turns the blood in my veins
To silt. I have no song, no hunger, joy or peace.
Put on your overshoes, my Fathers' hallowed plains,
You – not at my request – wrested from the seas.

chronisch / chronic

What Dutch sounds like to my English-speaking friends:

> Throaty, phlegmy, a little bit spitty.

> Guttural.

> A German who has to clear his throat.

> A French accent.

> German. Old English.

> Hebrew.

> Gentle French.

> A German-Swedish-Icelandic mix.

> Peaceful.

Solemn and respectful.

A friendlier German.

Rolling water against rocks.

Cold water pulls at the vowels.

Sounds break over the rocks, and fall back to the sea.

Rolling tongue.

An English recording played backwards.

Raw and sharp and smooth and round.

A clawed creature scrambling on a smooth steep slope

Harsh and halting.

Unhappy.

Brown and grey.

Phlegmy, and absent of emotion.

Like winter.

A dory out on choppy waters.

Lonely, forlorn.

Gentle, maternal.

Like it ought to be familiar.

Heavy with meaning.

Wind that gets caught in a tight space.

Tone is earthly.

Familiar, but then confusing.

Back of the throat, phlegmy.

Babbling and random.

Back of the throat.

Lots of endings with *t* and *k*.

Like socialism.

Like the smell of strong coffee, the splat of butter in a griddle.

Snow.

Someone clearing their throat on a foggy night.

Gurgling.

Leaves a salty taste in the mouth.

Something ancient, from the middle earth,
like the language of elves.

Phlegmy.

draak / dragon

My middle brother said he'd heard a physicist describe a way to visualize time as every motion that you'd ever made, in continuity, forming a sort of snake.

I tried to see it. We were in a park where I had often been, and I imagined the pattern of my activities there over the years: opaque where they were repeated, translucent where they were not—the walking movements, progressing forward, the smaller hand gestures reaching and returning in dead ends—and at home, the dense intertwinings in the kitchen, the heavy imprint of lying in bed. The loops of hiked trails. The long, vague residues made in a narrow chair over the Atlantic. That whole strange tube, that complicated snake, overlapping with millions of other people's snakes, with movements made seconds or millennia apart.

Eventually, it became too large for me to hold in my mind, bursting as if it had been an apparition. The two of us were in the park, standing between snowbanks, hunched into our winter coats.

I feel that same sense of the impossible when I try to picture language.

A galaxy? The stars are words. A vast smudge of them, a field of crowds and outliers, of older and newer entities. The words are clustered, but fluidly; they may belong in more than one constellation, according to sonics, or synonymy, or common origins.

Our minds can move these stars. We use grammatical or gravitational conventions. Each star is an idea with three presences—a sound, a symbol, a meaning—except in the galaxies without text. And we live in the stars, and we pass them around, and they remain essential and inadequate.

What I mean to say is that when I was young and traded one galaxy for another, there was a shift in the firmament that hasn't quite subsided.

We went to the imigration. In the office there, my brother and me started having funny stories and laughing. When I wrote this in a grade school journal, it was in the middle of a great transition; knowing that Dutch formulations wouldn't work, while still guessing at what English wanted. I had an English as a Second Language teacher, Mrs. Turnpenny, who was very precise. She taught us that Halloween was a contraction of Hallow's Evening, and made sure we knew the difference between a cauldron and a pot. She showed us pictures of the parliament buildings and Karen Kain.

At that stage of learning, when understanding English was still far from automatic, a literal interpretation of each word was inevitable; every time I heard or spoke the teacher's name, I saw a shiny penny flipping in slow motion through the air. She had us draw a schematic version of the leaf on that brown coin—eleven points above a stem—on red construction paper, for the room's white cinderblock wall.

In our small class, I was the only student whose galaxies overlapped. I was making subtle shifts in intonation, writing vaguely familiar words with trusted letters. In my cursive, I had to make only two changes. The lower case t, in English, was a stick that had to be crossed after the word was done. The Dutch t, in its self-containment, confused my teachers; they thought it was an f. The English capital I resembled a lower case l, so I abandoned the Dutch one, which looked like a tall y with its tail resting on the line.

The other students spoke Cantonese. Their route to literacy had involved learning thousands of characters; now they had to reconfigure their listening, their speech, the direction of their reading, the writing movements of their hands. I remember Tommy, a cheerful boy in a powder-blue track suit, exclaiming "this is so messy," when the teacher brought him a sentence to translate from Chinese script. That comment quietly astonished me—it was the sudden awareness that my unfamiliarity had dimensions; not only were those rows of enigmatic characters indecipherable to me, but I couldn't even tell that they were poorly drawn.

It was a relief to be in school. We had arrived early in the summer, and for a while, everything had felt starkly foreign; not only the Canadian English that emanated in limp convergences from the mouths of our neighbours—they barely seemed to move their lips when they spoke—but also the facial expression of the electrical sockets (surprised dismay), and the sound of ambulance sirens (a kind of wail that erupted and subsided in lamenting waves). The smell of rooms; drywall instead of plaster. The sidewalks made of large concrete pads laid out in a simple row. The sunlight, softer, more yellow, shorter-lived. The air was dense with humidity, bread was gluey, milk came inexplicably in plastic bags. Our linguistic disorientation, then, was part of a larger dissonance. Bread was not *brood*, and milk was not *melk*. We let the English percolate, watching Mr. Dressup on television, finding the library, playing outside and receiving practical instruction from the other children on the street. Run! Hide! You're it!

I had priorities of which I didn't fully grasp the implications. I was dimly aware that I'd fallen from power. In our old neighbourhood, I'd been one of the older children, and was often the one to devise the framework of play and assign the roles. None of that authority rested naturally in the physical; I was clumsy and asthmatic, and mostly afraid of the trajectories of soccer balls, the height of drainpipes, the hardness of pavement. My command had really been of the language; the others listened to me because I could conjure, order, deride, and amuse.

In Canada, my clothes were odd, and I had no idea what malls or Cabbage Patch Kids or gimp bracelets were, and when I tried to be funny with my peers the silences were awkward and prolonged. I felt an urgent wish to restore my own significance. I read everything I could—flyers, packaging, signs—and listened to the mumblings of my classmates and teachers. Willing myself to make the same sounds, I strove to regain a sense of fluency, of language as my element. That was all I had in my sights; it didn't occur to me that this was also the start of a slow and nebulous loss.

When we returned to our home in the Netherlands for a year, the English teacher winced at how I spoke. "It's awnt, not ant," she enunciated, "you're not the niece of an insect. Par-tee, not pardy." But I knew better. Her snake of time was curled inside our continent, and would remain, but mine had taken unexpected and disorienting flight to a country where people spoke English as I did.

elders / elsewhere

In Harrowsmith, Ontario, I once heard Robert Lovelace speak to an audience of farmers at the annual gathering of their Union. He placed a map of Canada and America on an overhead projector. The land was divided into irregularly shaped regions that were embedded within and against one another—nothing like the long, straight edges of the provinces and states. He explained that we were looking at bioregions: coastal forests, sand pine scrub, grass-land, alpine forests, taiga, and more. Then he laid a second map over the first, which appeared to dupli-cate the regions—but this, he said, was a map of Indigenous languages.

That revelation took slow hold inside of me. If languages existed within particular ecosystems, was that because their speakers inhabited those limits, and plateau scrubland people would not—could not, perhaps, given the knowledge and practices required for each to live—be sage and chaparral peo-ple? Or was there an influence of origins at work, an onomatopoeic element, with ecologically ambient sounds and forms giving rise to each language? I turned those questions over, asked them of friends; it compelled me that there was an inherent unity at work, a junction between land and word.

Months later, an insight arrived. I had grown up in such a language—my Dutch was of its land, while English, where I had learned it, was an invasive species imposed by settlers. My own ancestors had been equally oppressive: in Indonesia, in Manhattan, in Suriname, in the Caribbean, and in South Africa, among other places. *Apartheid*, the euphemism that means separateness, is perhaps the most internationally recognized Dutch word. Of South Africa's eleven official languages, Afrikaans—the independent language that formed during colonial occupation, merging Dutch with influences from Khoikhoi, Malaysian, Portuguese, German and French—was at first considered a dialect between owners and slaves. My language was unequivocally guilty, but it also mattered that I'd acquired it on the flat turf of its formation.

Until then I had attributed the sense of detachment I experienced in English, that sensation of having a tongue infused with lidocaine, to the language's belated integration in my life. Now I was in doubt; perhaps English felt less real because I was speaking it on the wrong land. Its sounds and constructs had nothing to do with the local earth, and neither did French—it was absurd for two languages to span such an enormous territory, and to sound so similar from the slopes of the Rockies to the coast of

New Brunswick. Names and terms had been placed on this land like a kind of linguistic asphalt; they didn't have to correlate with what was underneath, they only had to be steamrolled down.

Waar ben ik (where am I?) was the question that burned in me on the night when we were driven by my father's cousin from Pearson airport onto a highway with more lanes and ramps than I had ever seen. Toronto, to start, but then: Scarborough, Finch, Kennedy, Alexmuir. When those sounds refer to the lands of the Mississaugas, Anishnabeg, Chippewa, Haudenosaunee and Wendat, perhaps they are doomed to have a disembodied quality, a ventriloquist trying to make the ground speak.

My first Canadian teacher, who had grown up swimming in the Don River before it became too toxic, told us that Toronto was "a Native word for the meeting place," and that Ontario meant "the beautiful water." I was intrigued, and did not recognize that he was also giving an implicit history lesson, present in the idea that "Native" was a single language without its own name, and looming large in his assumption that no child in the classroom might have spoken the language, or held it in their family history. A genocidal impulse persists in the pretence that a genocide has been accomplished.

flits / flash

Dutch is not the name of my language.

Dutch, that crushed stone, that steaming pressure cooker valve, there is no resonance in that disintegrating syllable, Dutch, Dutch, Dutch—its closest correlate is *Duits*, which means German, which is altogether different, with is cragginess and hushings and reverently capitalized nouns.

The language I speak is *Nederlands, NAY-der-lahnts*, in three descending pitches. Of the lowland; low or humble or meek, as in the Sermon on the Mount, for they shall inherit the earth.

The utterances of my people, who used to dwell on hillocks, lone islands in the floodplains of the sea. And they had never heard of Christ.

When the tide was high, their houses looked like anchored ships.

In storms, the rains and whitecaps lashed their walls. Was it any wonder that the words they made would sound like phlegm? Their grooved hands gathered frigid peat, and dried it in the wind to make the slabs that fuelled fires. Rainwater was stored, for drinking, in a hole outside the door.

That is my language, of wind moving over earthen homes in shallow seas, of a vessel dipped in a rainwater pit, of a cough from a straw bed.

Consonants are land; vowels are water.

My speech of the sluiced and siphoned vowels. Of the proper vowels in straight trenches. Of the flat and stubborn vowels that will not stop seeping through the clay.

Grammar of nettles and elderberry and the speckled shells of seagull eggs. Of windbreaks of knotted willows. Of rivers that flood the fields and freeze. Irregular verb of wooden skates, the scrape of blades that herringbone the ice, the sensation of flying toward a flat horizon.

Crowded syntax of bicycles, released with the green light, a wheeling cluster that crests like a wave over an old arched bridge. The chirp of the signal for pedestrians with visual impairments, the swoosh of plastic rain-pant legs, the lingering, quietly stale flavour of coffee, and the salty aftertaste of bami goreng.

Disappearing dialects of fine terroir; of cities, twenty minutes apart, with distinct municipal accents. The verbal tunes of Drenthe, of Limburg, of Zwolle and Brugge and Rotterdam.

My vocabulary of images from a train at dusk; a reel of domestic scenes in the apartments near the tracks. A newspaper held wide by an unseen reader, an old man without a shirt, two children looking out. The clatter of the elevated rails.

Then indigo countryside, and one rural house, a solitary square of light.

That script of intimate and irretrievable moments in rooms, of living Polaroids, embedded in an immense and deepening darkness.

I speak the language of that train, and those apartments, and that house.

The syllabics of stairwells that smell of ammonia, of a sparse lawn where a woman in curlers holds the leash of her tiny dog, of a snack bar where the air is thick with deep-fryer fumes.

The diction of the lone house, with its straw roof and tile floors, the neighbouring medieval castle with a moat. Of waking to the calls of mourning doves and distant cows, lifting warm eggs from the dim coop, inhaling a forest of bark and mushrooms, sensing the discreet and sniffling progress of a hedgehog.

The sentence of the narrow road, bricks laid across from edge to edge, its rounded surface undulant. Bright moss growing in the seams. Pebbles and beech nuts pressed into the mortar dirt. The cadence of car tires, creaking and peaceful, a sound that swells until the bend, then coarsens and resumes.

I didn't know how deeply I'd absorbed the rolling sentence of that road until I was in labour, in

Canada—then it returned to me, not as an image or a recollection, but as an experience; it was night, and I was in bed, and a contraction would come, and when it eased I was a passenger on that brick road. I saw the trunks of the tall oaks alongside, the shafts of filtered sunlight between them, and I felt the slight rumble of the engine, but most of all I could hear the tires, that murmuring crescendo of approach, the crackle of splitting acorns, the steady rise in pitch before the turn. Then a contraction would eclipse the scene, and when it was over I'd be in the car again, on the road from Heino. The cycle seemed to go on for hours, and had an anchoring effect, but also made me melancholy; I wanted to tell my partner and the midwife, but the words felt unreachable—no one else spoke that language within a language.

My private *Nederlands*. My language of the inexpressible, of the confidential sections of my journal, of the inner territory between world and word.

gastarbeider / guest labourer

The month is May. I have not lived in the Netherlands for twenty-seven years. I haven't visited in a decade.

Er is geen tijd. Of is er niets dan tijd?

There is no time. Or is there nothing but time?

This is the closing line of *Eb*, by M. Vasalis. In the city of Leiden, along the Doelensteeg, her poem is painted on the outer wall of a house. I am 5,745 kilometers away from that tribute, near Lake Ontario, and this morning I'll read the poem out loud as a contribution to an art exhibit. I want to do it because I like the project's premise, and the artists are kind and curious, and seeing the movie *Pina* about the dancer Pina Bausch has left me with a latent wish to try performance art. My first objective is to accept the camera's gaze without armour; meaning, in this case, I do not make any effort to evoke feminine beauty. I wear no jewelry, leave my hair alone, and alter nothing of my face—I don't even look in a mirror to see if I have remnants of breakfast in my teeth.

It's not an ordinary reading. The poem, in this context, is only a vessel for sound. I will be filmed as I read the words, slowly elongating and repeating the vowels and consonants, shifting their sequence and pitch, playing with them until they lose meaning, and are simply sonic elements of Dutch.

We're in a large rehearsal room, with a view of the lake and an island. One of the artists stands behind the camera, while the other holds a fuzzy microphone high over my head. As I start to speak, I'm only making sense to myself—or not entirely; I feel the presence of a ghostly audience, millions of strangers with whom I have this lexicon in common. I sense the potential for a lie—if I had the skill to utter a plausible faux-Dutch, no one would know—but the requested degree of performance is enough for me; I read the poem. I can't seem to undo the words from their meaning:

Dit is de tijd die niet verloren gaat:

This is the time that is not lost:

Ik ben een oceaan van wachten,

I am an ocean of waiting,

My mind, in between the usual distractions and preoccupations, goes to some unexpected places as I repeat the lines.

I'm on the immense beach at IJmuiden, my words obliterated in the wind. After Vasalis died, her family released her unpublished poems in a collection called *De oude kustlijn* (The old coastline). She had chosen the title herself, based on her father pointing at some seabirds flying in a line and explaining that in the altered landscape, they still followed a former coast.

Then I'm in a plastic chair in my first Canadian classroom, watching the teacher write an example of a phrase in quotation marks on the board; all the sounds that I was trying to supress or eliminate then, I'm now setting free in this high-ceilinged room, as if for no other reason than to resurrect them.

"Never erase, it doesn't really work," my favourite art teacher said to me once, and I've learned she was right; the sound of Dutch persists like a faint carbon shadow in my English. It deepens after I've spoken to my mother, or when I'm breathlessly eager to recount something, or when I speak of anything that happened "over there." Very rarely, people guess my linguistic origins—once it was a man who had asked for spare change, and then heard me apologize and wish him good luck.

Back in the rehearsal room, I let go of coherence. Even in a context where no one understands the words, this feels like a vulnerability. Now I am no longer wearing the virtue of articulateness; I could be a bleating sheep. I think of my mother and her Dutch immigrant friends; how even after decades, the vowels in their English remain so *Nederlands,* especially the a that occurs, for example, in sad, or lack, or basket. Sedt, lek, bah-skit. Perhaps they avoid that long, brassy, forceful a not because they cannot form it, but because the making of that sound, its open-mouthed resonance, is undignified to a Dutch sensibility.

My syllables break down, and the effect is estranging. If this is my mother tongue, then why do I feel so constrained? For the first time, I hear what others have said of Dutch: it sounds harsh, guttural, staccato. I collide with the dead ends of consonants, the brief percussion of *t*, the choking *k*. The vowels, I find, are made to be short and contained—drawing them out, or fluctuating pitch, reveals their lack of fluidity. Standing there, half tongue-tied, the sounds that usually enliven me start to seem arbitrary and broken.

This reminds me of something that would happen occasionally in the years after we immigrated. In crowded places, like at stores or parties, where I was surrounded by people speaking English, the language would abruptly sound foreign again; it would take a few seconds to recover into comprehension.

Consonants are the body; vowels are breath. Breath in Dutch is *adem*, from the Sankskrit word for eternal self, or soul. The older meanings of the English term are steam, exhalation, and odour.

We move the air using our mouth, tongue and throat in particular, repetitive ways. It is possible, then, that our languages shape our faces; surely, they define an everyday expressive range, a sort of muscular vocabulary. And if that is a dance, then the Dutch choreography is terse, emphatic, and controlled.

"I loved to dance because I was scared to speak," Pina Bausch said of her German childhood.

I was vocal with familiar people as a child, but I deeply distrusted speaking to strangers. One afternoon, left for a haircut while my mother rushed to get groceries, I peed in the chair. A muteness had come over me, and I couldn't bring myself to ask for the bathroom. Part of what silenced me was the disruption that I could cause in the fabric of things; my fluency in Dutch was unexpected, and subject to interrogation or praise, neither of which were benign.

Recently, I learned of the work of linguist and logotherapist Manuela Julien. She teaches immigrant families in the Netherlands, who are often implicitly or otherwise discouraged from speaking their first language, that a thorough grounding in their mother tongue will actually improve their children's ability to learn Dutch once they start attending school. Julien also objects to the stigma inherent in the term *taalachterstand,* or language-behindness, which is used in her field to refer to these children's partially bilingual states.

There is a tension between the circumstances that Julien's work addresses and my own past. Three decades ago, I received negative attention for speaking Dutch too well, as if my fluency was an incursion, while the children she now works with are pathologized for not speaking Dutch well enough. I am still not sure where, between those polarities, Dutch children of colour might find their place of belonging.

The artists' exhibition is called *The Golden USB*; it presents samples from a catalogue of everything on earth, for the purpose of interstellar trade. At the gallery, the looped video of my reading is an item in the catalogue: "The Reproduction of Vibratory Patterns, Pitches and Types of Sounds Found in the Dutch Language." The screen is large, and my face enormous. A woman in a red dress stands in front of it, observing, then turns to her friend to say "What the hell!?" I force myself to watch myself. I look almost devotionally earnest, wearing a black shirt, and the fragments of sounds that my mother ingrained in me.

There is a Dutch word for a sense of inner, private amusement—*binnenpret*. On the way home, I feel this about the manner in which the project takes my childhood transgression to its limits; I am the intergalactic representative of the language that I wasn't supposed to speak or love. In the film, it has been reduced to pieces, momentarily defused.

heimwee / homesick

In my late twenties, I traverse the Netherlands with my anglophone partner, making introductions and translations. Underneath the levity of explaining menu items such as *koffie verkeerd* (coffee wrong; made with an excess of warm milk), or *patatje oorlog* (french fries war; with peanut sauce, mayonnaise and raw onions), I feel as if I'm doing something elemental, like weaving: love, this is my Beppe, these are my childhood friends, this was our house—land, this is the one I'll have children with.

It is early on New Year's Day when we start for home. We've celebrated *Oud en Nieuw* with friends who spoke a determined and endearing English, intoning every sentence as a question, and who made the traditional yeast donuts called *oliebollen* (oil-balls), sugared as if left out in a light snowfall. We've played cards. On this trip, I've noticed a new English word in the Dutch vocabulary: *relaxed*, pronounced rrre-lekst. A term of approval, meaning cool or enjoyable or laid back. The evening was relaxed.

At midnight, we stepped outside, and then everyone in the city lit their fireworks all at once. There were the classic firecrackers that soared and broke in slow, mesmeric stars, but also ones that snaked wildly along the street, or boomed without any light. A little girl with pigtails held a wand straight out in front of her, and it sprayed orange sparks along the surface of the street. Another firecracker went up with a long, high-pitched wail: "screaming kitchen-maid," I translated—*gillende keukenmeid*, and the eccentric term was like a forgotten trinket, retrieved from the back of a drawer in my mind.

Now the city streets are deserted, littered with firecracker debris. Outside of the train station, a chartered bus has pulled in. Its door opens and passengers file out. Neo-nazis. Cold and exhausted teenagers and young adults, gathering in huddles, crouching on the curb and lighting cigarettes behind cupped hands. They wear white pride badges on their jackets, or the number 88. The girls have platinum blonde hair. One skinny boy has *War!* etched on the back of his scalp.

We haul our bags into the station, giving the group wide berth. I try to observe them without making eye contact, but no one pays us any attention; they're too tired and hung-over. The bus driver sits behind an enormous convex windshield. He is staring straight ahead with an expression that is half shock and half sorrow. He has a thick, black moustache and brown skin.

We say goodbye to our friends, climb the tall stairs that cross the tracks, and buy our tickets from a vending machine. There's no one around. We board the waiting train, stash our bags away, and sit in the tall, paired seats. We're still finding words for the situation—the sight of those young skinheads, their apparent right to assemble, the lack of commentary from my friends—when one of the neo-nazis enters our train car.

He is lanky, dressed in black denim, and he moves around the empty compartment as if newly caged, clambering between seats, slamming on windows, laughing a few times before dialling a number on his cell. The train starts to move.

The skinhead, in his series of calls, could be speaking to people or machines; it's hard to tell. He shouts, punctuating his statements with English profanities. He has been at a concert across the border. It was awesome. He was kicked off the bus for driving people crazy. He thinks that was unfair, but also funny. He wants to meet his friends for beer.

Between calls, he moves in and out of different seats, then leans over the backrests in front of us, and asks how we're doing. His nose is running and his pupils are wide. I make an instinctive decision; right now, I can't be Dutch. I let my partner answer in English, grateful for the cover of his whiteness, his steady voice, and quiet physical strength.

The skinhead turns friendlier and switches to English himself. And where are we from, he asks. He tells us he likes Canadians. The train pulls into a station and he jumps up and bangs his fists on the windows, shouting at a woman on the platform: *hey slut, want to fuck?*

No one else comes in. My partner and I can't talk to each other without the skinhead noticing, but I know we're having similar thoughts: he is unstable, he could have a knife, there seems to be another passenger who is sitting alone, and there's a plane to catch. We do our best not to provoke him, not even by hauling our bags down and heading for another train car.

He lurches around the seats, texting and phoning, and then at the junction station, he leaves the train. Now we can speak, but we don't. I'm looking out at a bright winter morning—fields, industrial silos, multiplying rails—but inside of me there's another territory, experiences that resist articulation.

There were some boys in my old neighbourhood—the word for them was *rotjongens*, a merger of rotten and boys—bike-riding vandals in vivid tracksuits. Some of their older brothers were skinheads. I knew to steer clear of the places where they hung out, but once in a while they would linger on the footbridge over the small canal near our house, and there would be no avoiding them.

Then my language of the dear diminutive changed its nature: *hoertje,* little whore. My language of the glorious compound word became a weapon: *vuilnisbakkenras*, the word for mongrel, which translates literally as garbage-can-race. The image I saw in my mind was not of dogs feeding on refuse, but of my brothers and I emerging from the bins as if that was our birthing.

There was a night when I stayed too late on a soccer pitch outside of our usual bounds. The *rot-jongens* drifted over from the bike sheds at the edge of the field and began shoving and tripping me. One boy had a lighter. Once I was on the ground, he threatened to set my hair on fire. He also had a girlfriend, and she kept giggling, telling him that he was mean; at first I mistook this for kindness, and then I understood that there was a game happening between them, and her protests were part of the game and had nothing to do with me. I remember that there were one or two solitary adults around, taking their evening walks with their dogs, and that they didn't intervene.

The boys got bored and let me go, but for years afterwards, that incident would figure in my dreams. They didn't really warrant that much fear, but I was too young to know that. I used to imagine punching them, and watching them reel and fall; that fiction almost restored my sense of dignity. It was a naïve version of violence—there was no blood or bruising, my hand never hurt, and things always ended with their remorse.

Two decades later in the airport train, the child whom I was feels tremblingly close, but I also sense that I have reconfigured. There is relief. I have a place to hide now; English is a shelter. And there is also disappointment in myself; I picture the bus driver's face, and silently repeat the reasons I had not to stop and speak to him, to give him a moment of contact with somebody who wasn't armoured in insignias of hate: there was my fear, my disbelief, my rushing for the train.

When our stop comes, we exit into a great hall. The scene seems much too ordinary; commuters holding briefcases, absorbed in their private worlds—it feels wrong for them to be so composed, like actors flawlessly performing their parts: white man waiting for a train, white woman striding towards an escalator, black man pulling a rolling suitcase. I want to stand in their way, place my hands on the shoulders of their winter coats and say, "This can't go on!" But of course, if I do that, an usher will appear, someone in uniform to remove me from the show.

And what "this" do I even mean?

I suppose that language failed me then, and fails me still.

Nederlands, where is your compound word for the brown driver of a chartered bus filled with sullen neo-nazis, or for twelve-year-olds who have come to call their own demons little-mongrel-cunts? *Allochtoon* (the Dutch term that generally refers to people of colour who are immigrants or descendants of immigrants in the Netherlands) won't do. *Rotjongens* won't do. If you are that animate, evolving language, if you're the medium of all our lives, you're going to have to find the words.

ik / l

Aah [1]
Bay
Say [2]
Day
A
F
Ghay [3]
Ha! [4]
E
Yay
Ka [5]
L
M
N
O
Pay
Ku [6]
Air [7]
S
Tay [8]
(U) [9]

Vay
Way 10
Ix
Egrec
Zet

1. Not the low, o-like aah that tastes of
tongue depressor. Making that sound,
the lower lip must widen, baring a few
bottom teeth. In an English aah, air flows
almost passively from the relaxed mouth,
but this *aah* involves a slight clenching of
the soft palate and lower jaw. The sound
is higher-pitched and more acute; it could
plausibly be emitted by someone who has
accidentally placed their hand in a fire.
Although for me, this vowel that resounds
through the Dutch word *water* evokes that
liquid element. The water is a spring creek
with a grass bottom, green fronds graceful-
ly raked inside its glassy current.

2. The sound of *c* is subtly finer than *s*. It is
sifted flour. There is a faint whistle in it,
which seemed to me as a child to have
something to do with the flavour of *citroen*
(lemon). *Citroen* was only an umlaut away
from *Citroën*, the car that an austere and
gentle friend of my mother's drove for
decades. When she gave us rides, there

wasn't the usual vehicular feeling of being in a small, upholstered room; it was less clear whether we were outdoors or indoors, with the traffic audible through the thin walls, and the drafts, and in what may or may not be an imagined memory, the sight of the blurred road through a seam at my feet.

3.   This notorious *ghay* has a guttural, scraping sound which exists in Arabic as well, but not in English. Imagine a porous k. In northern Dutch, the letter originates in the throat; the windpipe tightens in a brief gargle. In southern Dutch and Flemish, the impetus is raised to the rear of the mouth, which tenses slightly during a quick burst of air. This *g* is known as a "soft g," which describes both its relative effect on the ear and its demand on the speaker's voice. Loud or frequent use of the northern pronunciation can lead to hoarseness, and in teachers' college my mother and her classmates were taught to use the soft g when lecturing. For me, this single phonetic substitution, this elevation of a sound within the throat, is enough to invoke the southern Dutch provinces: saints, white farmhouses, fruit pies with glazed ribbon crusts. Trying to sleep at a friend's house in Maastricht, while the music next door plays much too loudly.

"I want to ask them to turn it down," the friend says, "but they'll never listen to me with my northern accent—I'll have to get my housemate to do it."

4. With the *aah* described in 1.

5. See 4. Crows look different in the Netherlands: smaller, punkish versions of the Ontario standard. I've listened, but it's hard to say which version of *aah* they favour in cawing, as they seem to possess a vowel range beyond our alphabet. Recent studies indicate that American and European crows do not understand the majority of each other's vocalizations.

6. See 9.

7. My last school year in the Netherlands was my first year of high school, and early on two processes occurred in enigmatic alliance. One was that I saw the girls in the grade ahead of ours transforming; we were all variously pubescent, but they were becoming womanly in their dress— they wore hoop earrings, and silk scarves, and boots with small heels. I understood that this awaited us. Part of me longed to be like them, and part of me wanted to remain in track pants, biking through

puddles just to generate the splashing wake. At the same time, the way those girls pronounced the letter *r* was changing, and I soon heard it among my friends—they were dampening the sound, holding back on the vibratory rolling of the tongue. I don't know where the transition started, but I followed willingly, and that new and enduring slant in our speech was a similar gesture, inexplicably, to wearing mascara.

8. This *t* is more percussive than the English one. It is the sound a cymbal makes when first struck.

9. In English, the vowel u starts with the consonant y, but in Dutch it is a *klinker* without a frame. Merge the u in pure into one short tone with the o in toque, while firmly constricting the lips and keeping the tongue low; that might be *u*. *U* is the only Dutch letter that's also a word; it is the formal you, the deferential counterpart to *jij*, and is used to address strangers and elders. *U* is generally a lower case word; the capitalized *U* is for those whom the speaker holds sacred, such as a monarch or god. At my grandparents' table, where the heaviest meal was still at noon, in rhythm with an obsolete agricultural day, the divine *U* was addressed as *Vader* (Father).

That was what my grandmother called my grandfather as well, and so a familial-theological conflation took place, as it would have in millions of other households at that same hour—though for me as a child it seemed to sanctify my Opa alone. Now I think of my Oma, with her ironed slacks, her acerbic remarks, her anxieties, and I wonder what life might have looked like if, over the steaming potatoes, we had prayed to her.

10. Inside the Dutch w is a very soft v. Say winter, vinter, winter, vinter, winter, vinter, until the difference disappears.

juli / July

It isn't far, from Dutch to English. On the tree of Indo-European languages, the two are almost neighbours; twigs growing from the West Germanic branch. Only the North Sea divides their founding lands from one another, its grey waters studded with oil rigs and wind turbines, inscribed with the wakes of freighters. Dutch fishermen used to call it the *haringvijver*, the herring-pond. Same alphabet. Same syntax in saying all roads lead to Rome: *alle wegen leiden naar Rome*.

I'd often looked out over the North Sea, from the beach itself, and from an apartment window, a heavy pair of binoculars pressed to my face. At the horizon, where flat cloud formations merged the sea with the sky and played shimmering visual tricks, I would convince myself that I could see England. I couldn't; due to the earth's curvature across the distance I was really staring at a slope of salt water.

My father's sister lived in England. One summer we took a ferry to visit her. The boat was massive, with an arcade and a daycare and a duty-free store, and was named for the royal house of Orange-Nassau. The opaque and churning furrow that trailed our ship gave me a sense of dread. I weighed it against the small, round life-buoys that hung from the railing and felt uncertain whether grown-ups had any real grasp on the circumstances.

There was an old nursery rhyme about England:

Zwarte zwanen, witte zwanen,
wie wil er mee naar Engeland varen?
Engeland is gesloten, de sleutel is gebroken.

Black swans, white swans,
who wants to come to England faring?
England is closed, the key is broken.

The lines were said to be based on a moment in the many wars between the two countries. The English had docked some of their navy on the Medway river and strung a metal chain across the water for protection. Eventually, the Dutch ship *Pro Patria* broke through the chain, or perhaps it was able to sail over it; the historical accounts differ. In any case, the Dutch fleet was victorious, and towed away the English flagship *The Royal Charles*—its stern carving can still be viewed at the *Rijksmuseum*.

On our trip, England was protected with a row of customs booths, like the ticket stalls at an amusement park. And they let us in.

I learned to sing my little cousin's favourite song to him, *Baa, baa, black sheep*. When we played cricket at the park, I dropped the ball, and another player yelled "Butterfingers!" It took me a minute to figure out the term, and then I marvelled at what it conveyed. Butter, pronounced with such rich, fatty emphasis. The almost whimsical indictment of my hands.

It's not that we hadn't heard English before. My father was from Kenya, where it was an official language, and we had been there several times.

It was also in the Harry Belafonte records that he played at home on the weekends.

"Mama, look a boo boo" they shout,
They mother tell them "Shut up your mout',"
"That is your daddy", "Oh, no,"
"My daddy can't be ugly so!"

Those lyrics made me sad, and I questioned if I was hearing them right. In retrospect, they named the unnameable, in a neighbourhood where our father was an isolated brown man, and racism could make our love for him feel like a nebulous vulnerability. Maybe that is why he felt drawn to repeat that song on the stereo. In those years, my parents argued in English; I strained to grasp hold what they were saying, and at the same time, I didn't want to know.

On the return crossing from England, my family and I were out on the ship's deck. As we passed one of the small, suspended lifeboats, I saw a man asleep inside.

"Kees!" I said.

He was my friend's father, who worked at the university, as my father did. At the sound of his name, he blinked his eyes open, and then he smiled very beautifully in recognition.

A few years later, Kees died of an aneurysm in his sleep. The song that closed his funeral was *No Expectations* by The Rolling Stones. English sounded so appropriate then, in that hall of stricken people, against the spectre of sudden loss. It was grand and worldly and for almost all of us, it bridged the familiar and the incomprehensible.

I find it easier to write about my friend's father than my own. There's the degree of remove, the definitive event, the facts that willingly condense into a paragraph. How do I distil what happened in our house?

During our last year in the Netherlands, and our first half decade or so in Canada, my father, who had been an enthusiastic and kind man, became depressed and furious. He took much of that out on me. I think he felt that what had been hostile to him in the Dutch culture was also embedded in my reluctance to emigrate, and then my homesickness. It was from him that I learned the word bitch. Meanwhile, my mother placed two weights on opposite sides of a scale: her marriage, her daughter—and I was too light.

Now, I possess the means to speak of what happened with insight: intergenerational trauma, internalized racism, displaced anger—the asbestos gloves needed to handle the scalding material. My parents and I can look at that past and then face each other again. But at the time, there was only pain and shame, aching slant rhymes. There was the dread of coming home from school.

I didn't want to mention that; I tried to contain where the words went, but there are submerged forces in writing—in the land-water realms of consonant-vowel—that require our surrender. My old landscape knows this: drained, dammed, channelled, pumped—a place where sailboats pass over a highway, where the sea has gates that are shut during storms, where farmers' ploughs can unearth a shipwreck—and still the living water finds its way. "A river does not let itself be pressed into a corset," says the book that celebrates 200 years of the Ministry of Infrastructure and Water Management, in reference to the Rijn. And so the stream underneath this fragment wills its direction; if I want the image of my friend's father, napping in a lifeboat, then its currents lead to my own *papa*, introducing me to British fish and chips when I still admired him without reserve.

Not long after Kees died, we left the Netherlands for good. That was how I came to encounter Lake Huron later that same summer, and its effect on me was an immediate and enormous longing for the North Sea. The drive to the water had resembled what I'd known: we'd gone west for about an hour, through flat, agricultural land, and then parked at the sand dunes of a beach that continued endlessly to the left and right. But here the air had no silt, and only smelled vaguely of weeds. The anemic waves, weak and irregular, lapped at the rough sand. No tide, no breath; a body of water in need of resuscitation.

The North Sea was an Atlantic inlet, and to me its shoreline held an ever-present sense of potential; although it was improbable, a whale or a freighter or a giant squid carcass could wash ashore, or an unknown seedpod, or a bottled letter from Tierra del Fuego. To be there was to press against the pulse of the entire world.

The lake looked empty and bland. I waded out into the cool, transparent water, farther and farther, but it came no higher than my waist. Later, on a cross-cut map, I saw that the shallow edges of Lake Huron were narrow, and the lake was really a plunging trough, deep as a bell-shaped flower. Perhaps wading into such a lake is like the process of learning English after Dutch. You start out on a sandy bottom and your footing is sure. You find words that are identical: water, land. Many others retain their similarities: *zee* and sea, *schip* and ship, *vader* and father, *vaarwel* and farewell. Even *branding* and breakers aren't entirely strangers. Then comes the plummet: *begrafenis* and funeral, *ramp* and disaster, *bladzij* and page. That's when you have to push off and swim.

kennis / knowledge

1 In the beginning created God the heaven and the earth.

2 The earth now was wild and void, and darkness was on the abyss; and the Spirit Gods hovered over the waters.

3 And God said: There be light! and there became light.

4 And God saw the light, that it good was; and God made separation between the light and between the darkness.

5 And God named the light day, and the darkness named He night. Then was it evening been, and it was morning been, the first day.

6 And God said: There be a firmament in the middle of the waters; and that make separation between waters and waters!

7 And God made that firmament, and made separation between the waters, that under the firmament are, and between the waters, that above the firmament are. And it was so.

8 And God named the firmament heaven. Then was it evening been, and it was morning been, the second day.

9 And God said: That the waters from under the heaven in a place assembled become, and that the dry seen become! And it was so.

10 And God named the dry earth, and the assembly of the waters named He seas; and God saw, that it good was.

11 And God said; that the earth shoot out grass-sprouts, herb seed-sowing after its nature, fertile trees, bearing fruit after their nature, which seed therein be on the earth! And it was so.

12 And the earth brought forth grass-sprouts, herb seed-sowing after its nature, and fruit-bearing trees, which seed therein was, after its nature. And God saw, that it good was.

13 Then was it evening been, and it was morning been, the third day.

14 And God said: That there lights are in the firmament of the heavens, for separation to make

between the day and between the night; and that they are for signs and for set times, and for days and years!

15 And that they are for lighting in the firmament of the heavens, for light to give on the earth! And it was so.

16 God then made those two great lights; that great light for governance of the days, and that small light for governance of the nights; also the stars.

17 And God set them in the firmament of the heavens, for light to give on the earth.

18 And for to rule on the day, and in the night, and for separation to make between the light and between the dark. And God saw, that it good was.

19 Then was it evening been, and it was morning been, the fourth day.

20 And God said: That the waters abundantly bring forth a teeming of living souls; and the fowl fly over the earth, in the firmament of the heavens!

21 And God created the great whales, and all living wriggling souls, which the waters abundantly brought forth, after her nature; and all winged fowl after their nature. And God saw, that it good was.

22 And God blessed them, saying: Be fertile, and multiply, and fulfill the waters in the seas; and the fowl multiplieth on the earth!

23 Then was it evening been, and was it morning been, the fifth day.

24 And God said; The earth bringeth living souls forth, after her nature, cattle, and crawling, and wild beasts of the earth, after their nature! And it was so.

25 And God made the wild beasts of the earth after their nature, and the cattle after their nature, and all the crawling beasts of the earth-bottom after their nature. And God saw, that it good was.

26 And God said: Let Us people make, after Our image, after Our likeness; and that they governance have over the fish of the sea, and over the fowl of the heaves, and over the cattle, and over the whole earth, and over all the crawling beasts, that on the earth crawl.

27 And God created the person after His image; after the image of God created He him; man and woman created He them.

28 And God blessed them, and God said unto them: Be fertile, and multiply, and fulfill the earth, and submit her, and have governance over the fish of the

sea, and over the fowl of the heavens, and over all the beasts, that on the earth crawl!

29 And God said: See, I have you-people all the seed-sowing herb given, that on the whole earth is, and all trees, in which seed-sowing tree-fruit is; it be you for victuals!

30 But to all the beasts of the earth, and to all the fowl of the heavens, and to all the crawling beasts of the earth, wherein a living soul is, have I all the green herb for victuals given. And it was so.

31 And God saw all what He made was, and sees, it was very good. Then was it evening been, and it was morning been, the sixth day.

liefde / love

After my family's migration, I copied poems from books—sometimes, if the font was especially pleasing, I even tore them out and taped them up over my bed, near the pillow, where the wall was closest to dreams.

My room was half underground in a suburb called Whitehills, my school was named for someone knighted by the British Queen, and the television that was my afternoon companion spoke a hypnotic, inflated American English, but the poems were in Dutch. I felt exposed, posting them there, in sight of my mother delivering clean laundry, or the odd friend coming by, but that discomfort was outweighed by the need to be near them. One of the poems, written in tight cursive lines on the inside of an old notebook cover, was Leo Vroman's *Vrede*.

> *Sinds ik mij zo onverwacht*
> *in een taxi had gestort,*
> *dat ik in de nacht een gat*
> *naliet dat steeds groter wordt,*

How to translate those concise, urgent lines, with their internal and end rhymes, their repetition of the rupturing g? In the attempt below, which is somewhat faithful rhythmically, the rhyme scheme has already changed from *abab* to *abba*. Given the syntax of English, I can't make the verb "left" trip into the fourth line, as it should to convey a frightened haste. "Widens constantly" is too formal; "keeps getting bigger" would be right.

> Since I so unexpectedly
> threw myself into a cab
> that in the night I left a gap
> behind that widens constantly

At thirteen, I not only loved the cadences of this poem; in accordance with that age's epicentric sense of self, I read my own experience into the quatrain. I felt it described what had happened to me when we emigrated.

Vroman's poetry flows from a playful, melancholic curiosity. He was an accomplished researcher in hematology; he elucidated a property of the blood's coagulation proteins that is still known as the "Vroman Effect." Residing for most of his postwar life in America, he wrote in one notorious poem that he "would rather have homesickness than Holland." A small number of his works, including *Vrede*, are like that—declarative and almost anthemically known—but the majority are gently surrealist, as enigmatic as fables.

At eighteen, I stayed in IJmuiden with my Friesian grandmother for a summer. It was a strange, lonely, and privileged time; there was a bureaucratic hitch that prevented my employment, but I had a place to stay, and a borrowed bike, and I drew or read or wheeled around, through the dunes, the dockyards, and the city.

Our family had not recovered from our immigration, but like many children and adolescents, I felt the pressure to reveal none of that turmoil to the outside world. My mother relayed cheerful fictions to our relatives and friends; she sensed that I was a potential leak in the vessel, and monitored the phone when I spoke to them. Our grief, our feelings of isolation and incompetence, the looming threats of poverty and failure, all the suppressed anxiety and sadness made the air in our home feel dense and treacherous to breathe.

I knew that I had to retrace our move in order to save myself. I was looking for something that summer in IJmuiden but I couldn't name it or find it. I was unhappy, but I also knew I was lucky to have the interval, to get so lost that I could let myself navigate on unknowable impulses: turn left at this brick street, stop at this bench, draw that person, follow that sky to the beach. It was an intuited existence, in which all motion seemed to lead eventually to the sea. The city was below a transatlantic flight path—I had seen the gullet of the canal from the airplane myself—and I imagined the passing jets as needles pulling threads of smoke, mending an impossible rupture.

Then a day happened that seemed to have a momentum of its own, a day like a great wave that lifted me up and deposited me further along in my life. I was sitting in a park at the edge of a wading pool where I'd often played as a child. I found a newspaper, and was scanning the classifieds for work that seemed casual enough to not require my missing documents, when I saw an improbable little ad; Leo Vroman would be reading that afternoon, almost three hours away, in a city where I'd never been. I knew him to be reclusive. I knew him to live in Texas. I had just enough money left to get there, so I locked up my bike and went.

The buses and trains all connected. I reached the reading venue, an arts centre along the languid Maas, with half an hour to spare. The downtown was upstream, cloaked in a warm haze, and from among its bridges and spires, brass band music came and went on the vagaries of the breeze. I watched the water's quiet pull. A slow, loaded barge—the sort of vessel that as children we had envied as a living space, with cheerful laundry hanging on a line, and toys on the front deck—came into view. The boat pushed the water ahead of itself in a smooth green ridge, and the graceful cursive name on the hull was my mother's; it would be contrived to write that in a story, but this was real life. At last, I had the breakthrough of feeling utterly at home.

Inside the building, a crowd in stylish, black garments had begun to gather, but I didn't mind my cords and old t-shirt. The tickets were free. When

Leo Vroman stood at the lectern, he was diminutive, but his face resembled Quentin Blake's rendition of the Big Friendly Giant. He read softly, with kindness. A number of poets from other countries read as well, each in their own languages, without translations. The sounds that came through the speakers were enigmatic and incantatory, almost like secular prayers.

The IJmuiden beach is wide as a void; at low tide, the walk to the water constitutes its own pilgrimage. The wind blows in from the sea, sometimes speaking the hollow, quickened syllables of flames, sometimes clamouring like a garage door rolling shut. The first stretch of sand is fine and deep. It rises in vapours and veils from the ground, and asks for effort from your legs. Then the ground dampens and darkens. There are shreds of washed-up kelp, an inky green, and thousands of razor shells—a carpet of deserted homes that require a deliberate, slowed planting of each footstep. The blades crunch and pulverize. Then comes the relief of rippled ground, the sand that's firm and ridged with lines that scroll as if in an endless, blurred cursive, the written version of Larkin's "something almost being said." The water arrives in thin, foamy, overlapping crescents. And there are stranded jellyfish of frosted blue glass, loose crab claws, and lone fish spines.

The rush of the sea in a conch is language; it is the sound removed from the thing. In that dissociation, space and time dissolve; the conch could speak of the sea, even far inland, and even after the sea had been turned into a field of sugar beets.

I have a postcard of IJmuiden's semaphore, which stands beside the lighthouse. Next to the iconic, red, squat tower, the semaphore looks futuristic and complex. On the path below is an ice cream cart, bearing the word *raket* in italicized capitals, for the rocket popsicle. When my mother was small, her father would bike out there with her. The semaphore spoke to the ships in coded flashes of light. And that, too, is embedded in language—in speaking, in writing, in our search for the words—the notion of an entity, out there on the waves, and our wish for them to receive the signal.

In one of his poems, *Voor Wie Dit Leest* (*For Whomever Reads This*, or *For Whomever Is Reading This*), Vroman addresses us directly to articulate his own tender gesture to the reader: "I'd like to be below this page / and through the letters of this poem / look into your reading face / and long for the melting of your pain."

Mio / Mio

When I was eight years old, and my youngest brother was four, my mother sent us on an errand. It may have been for cheese or bread or meat. There were separate stores for each of those. The bread could be ordered white or brown, sliced or not, and round or cut— the sort of cut done with scissors, *geknipt*, not with a knife, *gesneden*, probably because the latter indicated a sliced loaf. Cut meant the baker had carved a line down the middle of the dough so that it rose in two parallel mounds and each slice looked like it had large mouse ears. I found this version more delicious.

On this day, there must have been some small item that held my brother's attention. When I turned around, he was half a block behind me, crouching and looking at the ground. I shouted "Zamir!" repeatedly until he came over.

At the same time, a man approached us from the direction of the shops. Perhaps he had been sitting on one of the benches, under which sparrows pecked at crumbs. He shuffled, and wore a rumpled brown suit, and his hair and moustache were dark gray.

"Zamir?" he asked, "Zamir?" He beamed at my brother as if a loss had been undone.

I could by then read some of the ethnic conventions of our town. A short man with formerly black hair, olive skin, and an old-fashioned suit was Turkish. Of course, I also knew the hollowness of that assumption; people called us Turks sometimes, and it was never a neutral term. Turkish immigrants were not a major presence in our neighbourhood, but lived in the apartments further south. I felt an allegiance and empathy with their status, an almost familial bond, and I also understood that it was detrimental to be mistaken for them. In the supermarket, where the eyes of some cashiers would track us with such vigilant, venomous, warning looks—a silent language that our mother was unaware of, and that I sensed would be impossible for me to translate—it was our resemblance to Turkish children that made them stare.

"Zamir," I confirmed, a little hesitantly.

The man asked me something, but not in Dutch. Then he fumbled in his pocket, pulled out a bar of white chocolate, partly eaten, and tried to give it to my brother. I held my breath. Here was the notorious stranger offering candy, but his gesture felt benevolent. I told my brother he could accept, as long as he didn't take a bite. The man rubbed Zamir's hair, and muttered his name again, and then I thanked him and we left.

Names are an intimate pocket within every language. There are no other words that we arrive at quite so purposefully and lovingly as the names we give our children. Nouns may lose specificity as we experience the world; bread is a rye slab, a rice flour loaf, a pale baguette, a slice from a bag; bread is money—but names burrow in the other direction; they progressively signify the close entities they represent. I don't mean that Zamir is a single, focused image—Zamir is decades of interactions: he is a child and teenager and adult, he has his son on his shoulders at a summer festival, a confiding way of saying his name on the phone, a range of insights, a biography. What I mean is that every new quality the word has taken on for me has to do with his existence.

We often lose our names when we emigrate; in earlier decades, some officials anglicized names without asking, and current immigrants may still choose to do so themselves. But even when our names remain the same, they are unlikely to be pronounced exactly as they were, or to be understood for their historical or cultural implications. I was twenty-eight years old when I learned that my first name is old-fashioned; a Toronto taxi driver, originally from Pakistan, asked if it bothered me. I told him that I had only ever lived in places where people encountered it as new.

I don't know if the man near the shops was moved to hear a familiar name in itself, or whether it suggested someone specific to him, but even then, before my own migration, his emotion of recognition was fathomable to me.

My favourite writer at that time was Astrid Lindgren. I don't think I ever considered that her work hadn't been written in Dutch. Her translator, Rita Verschuur, later recalled Lindgren's encouragement and instruction: "As long as the tone is right." Her books were immersive to me. I was relieved to find, on our weekly trips to the library, that I hadn't reached the end of them.

We had an attic, where laundry was hung and some items were stored, and when I curled under its slanted roof with any one of her books and a few provisions—apples, nuts, raisins—and heard the vague noises of my family below, and rain drumming overhead, I felt a sense of utter contentment, an ideal balance of shelter and abandon.

When playing outside, I liked to assign the other children names from Lindgren's writing: Rasmus, Olle, Gunnar, Britta. The book I loved most of all was about a lonely boy named Bosse, who was transported to a magical land, where he learned that his real name was Mio, and he was the King's son. The title of that book, *Mio, My Mio*, was almost too beautiful to say out loud. Recently, I looked up the English translation and found it was called *Mio, My Son*. I missed the mesmeric repetition of that name.

At first, in Canada, I found English names very hard to retain. They were empty labels, strangely alike, and I made an effort to give them narrative moorings. Brent, the boy on the corner with smooth glossy hair and a sneaky-sounding laugh. A fast name, with the Dutch word for "run" in it. Kimmy, the girl up the street with a boat in the garage and cheerfully large teeth. With a soft k, with a muffled y.

And what would I have done if I had met a child, in those vertiginous months of adjustment, who was named Joppe, like my oldest friend? I probably would have felt a sudden affection, and wanted to approach him, and confirm the realness of his hair.

That long gone day with my brother, we did the shopping and walked home. My mother inspected and approved the chocolate bar, and we argued, Zamir and I, over whether it was his or ours.

natuur / nature

I once received a small wooden box that seemed flaw-lessly made. Holding it now makes me think of the poems of Ida Gerhardt, the Dutch poet and classicist whose life spanned most of the twentieth century. The dovetailed corners, flush edges, little click of the closing lid—they are the material equivalent of her verses, assembled with the same proficiency that she brought to metre, diction, pacing, and rhyme.

But the box alone does not convey the compressed power of her work—not the way that I use it, for stones and small notes from friends. If it could hold a fragment of turbulent weather instead, a torrent of rain or a gale, that would be a Gerhardt poem. Her craft resonates with her own religious upbringing; the forms are Calvinism's stern restraint, a spiritual framework tight as a quatrain, through which great forces and concepts pass.

Although she lived for years in voluntary exile, Gerhardt's writing was so *Nederlands*, so utterly inti-mate with the Dutch language and landscape, that I find it resistant to translation. She left almost no room between structure and subject. "After the dark-bronze striking of the hour," she wrote of a church tower's bell. In another poem, she repeats the phrase "Wij geven de waterstand"—the radio's standard report of the water levels in her region. The monument to her poetry is in the ideal spirit; two plaques on the edge of the Merwede river inscribed with her poem *Text on a River Beacon* and embedded in the ground beside an actual, operating beacon. Out past the words, there is river and sky and field. *Een lucht van geweld*, she once wrote of an impending storm over her town: "a sky of violence."

Much of her writing had ominous undertones, but she also wrote a poem that is still widely invoked in the Netherlands for comfort after a death; *De Gestorvene* (*The Deceased,* in the singular). The poem's speaker declares that they would travel seven times around the earth, if necessary on their hands and feet, to greet "that one" who would be "standing there laughing and waiting." As an adolescent, I loved the merger of almost unbearably grand emotion with practical detail—lines that translate something like, "clothes in tatters / what would it matter."

Biografisch I

De taal slaapt in een syllabe
en zoekt moedergrond om te aarden.

Vijf jaren oud is genoeg.
Toen mijn vader, die ik het vroeg,

mij zeide: 'dat is een grondel',
—en ik zàg hem, zwart in de sloot—

legde hij het woord in mij te vondeling,
open en bloot.

Waarvoor ik moest zorgen,
met mijn leven moest borgen:

totaan mijn dood.

Biographical I

The language sleeps in a syllable
and seeks motherground to earth.

Five years is old enough.
When my father, whom I asked,

said to me: "that is a gudgeon,"
—and I *saw* it, black in the creek—

he laid that word in me as foundling,
open and exposed.

For which I had to care,
with my life secure,

unto my death.

I've translated Gerhardt's lines as straightforwardly as I could, but the result fails to convey their music. The original work has a rhyme scheme—$a_1 a_2$ b b c_1 d c_2 d e e d, with the first numbered pair signifying assonance, and the second a semi-rhyme—and nothing has come of the hours that I've tried to reproduce it because I can't reconfigure the closing line on which things hinge; it has to end with death.

In English, death has a rare sound, and the only ordinary word that rhymes with it is breath, which is a rather lovely grouping. But the Dutch *dood* is common, it can rhyme with bread and gutter and boat and Jew and nut and whistled and lead and lap and bump. Death won't rhyme with "creek" or with "naked," the literal meaning of the word I translated as "exposed," which I chose because "open en bloot" form a customary phrase, like "open and exposed."

Furthermore, *Biographical I* doesn't simply have a rhyme scheme; it has a complex sonic landscape with subtle inner resonances that amplify its meaning. I can't articulate exactly the significance of how the long *aa* sounds in the first two stanzas, in *taal* and *slaapt* and *syllabe*, and *aarden* and *jaren* and *vader*, are a foundation for the short *a* sound that occurs only in the third stanza of epiphany, of the father's words and the speaker's seeing, except to say that something in the structure had to declare that instant, to mark it as immediate and formative.

It's true that Gerhardt is mythologizing her own task in this poem—as a designated guardian of the word, the profoundly Dutch word that lives in the water (and is a vowel away from *grendel,* the latch or bolt of a door)—but I admire that, because no one else would have done it for her, this notoriously uncompromising woman, who was reclusive, covertly lesbian, and whose poetry was not widely acclaimed until late in her career; she was from an era where she had to fight even to have her name on the cover of her first collection, as the publisher wanted to list it only on the title page.

And so, when I say that I get this poem, that it speaks to me of the mysteriously foundational level where my own work originates, I know that I am staking a vicarious claim in that mythology, and I won't apologize. *Five years is old enough*; but unlike Gerhardt, I do not write in the language that I was given then.

This complicates the undertaking.

Sometimes I translate my own poems, in either direction (I was going to write, forwards or backwards). It's a private little exercise, the taking apart of a gadget, to see what happens when I reassemble it. One of my English poems contained the word harbour, which for me conjures a generic image; there are ships, docks, and gulls, but it is nowhere that I can name. When I replaced it with the Dutch word *haven*, the picture was immediately distinct. I saw our former river harbour, a charmless place of silos and concrete piers, where St. Nicholas arrived on a boat each year in November, with his cohort of *Zwarte Pieten*; white people shamefully performing in blackface, speaking an invented Dutch. *Haven* was a bicycle ride on an overcast afternoon, during which my youngest brother sat in a seat on my father's handlebars. I was being somewhat reckless, biking in a slalom between the moorings, near the sheer drop to the water. My brother told me to stop, and then he repeated himself so desperately that I suddenly knew he loved me.

Haven made contact with that epiphany, and harbour did not; only the mother tongue's term remained resonant with the primacy of experience. That knowledge frightened me. Could I write in a language that wouldn't channel my earlier selves?

The answer evolves as I work. Translating my own English lines becomes more than a game; when I am reminded of the depth of *haven*, my ghosts enter the poem. And I am not in this alone—I'm doing what millions of others also have to do: making a life in the other tongue, writing and speaking as if to strike new sparks between English and myself.

For this, there may be a method embedded in Gerhardt's own advice to translators; of her translation of Lucretius' *On the Nature of Things*, she wrote, "The translator will, against the sonorous Latin verse, constantly experience a certain *patrii sermonis egestas* (inadequacy of the mother tongue). No other option remains for him [sic], except to listen attentively—ever more attentively, more sharply—until that listening puts the own language to work."

English is not my mother tongue, but it has adopted me. If I listen closely enough against the soundscape of my former language, I trust that it will start to work.

That deep listening is not only to speech—although there, too, it is an essential and subtle process. I used to give private Dutch lessons in Canada, and would have students practice the three diphthongs, *ui*, *eu*, and *ij*. Some made them sound entirely alike, and I mistook this for a difficulty in pronunciation. I'd demonstrate, exaggerating the shaping of the mouth. Then one day a young boy said in frustration: "But they sound exactly the same!" I realized then that the trouble was in the tuning of the ear.

Past the words, there is the listening to place. To the thaw of the ice on a Great Lake; to the call of a loon; to the chimes of closing subway doors; to clothes tumbling in rows of dryers.

Gerhardt put it like this: "If I in this land / might have a spell *alone* / then the water's edge / would surely write the book for me." Reading that, I day-dream of orchestrating a ghostly meeting between her and Mary Oliver (a fellow admirer of Lucretius), who said simply, "Listening to the world. Well, I did that, and I still do it."

oud / old

Returning from exile at sunrise, my dual longing is for words and for landscape. I savour the terse welcome from the customs officer, the accumulation of overheard phrases in the arrivals hall and on the station platform, and then the train window's view of that wide, flat green.

The countryside is linear and disciplined; nature in the governance of engineers. As a child on road trips, I would sometimes experience an illusion of scale; the sense that I was large enough to reach out my gigantic hand and tenderly stroke the landscape as it passed. Now, from the train, it's almost as if language rises like a vapour, an early morning fog that fills the drainage creeks and blankets the tilled soil, and might drift to reveal the otherworldly dance of a stork, that clicking bird whose name is all long vowels and soft consonants, *ooievaar*. Then English suddenly feels awkward and contrived; a dream I've had in which my tongue didn't work quite right.

On my most recent visit, after an interval of eleven years, there were new graves for me to kneel at; people whom I loved, passed into immobile entropy, disintegrating in the thick, clay ground. Something of their deaths felt familiar; I think that was because, in the first few years after emigrating, I had attempted a sort of psychic killing of everyone we'd left behind.

This made for an odd form of comfort: yes, I had lost them, but that was all—if they were dead, then what I hadn't lost were actual, available minutes or hours or years in their presence. When people called us, they ruined this illusion. I hurt the living dead by refusing to come to the phone. If they were there and I was not—if my grandparents were sitting in the same upholstered chairs at the same picture window, filling out crosswords and smelling faintly of juniper soap, if my friends were pausing in their usual afternoons, twisting the phone cord on a breather from their bicycling, irreverent collectives—one flight away, one half-day away—well, that was unendurable.

I later found a reference to such a method in a short story by Steven Heighton, in which a fictional textbook defines the Japanese word *omoikiru*:

> *For example: To see again those I have cared for is impossible; there is no help for it but to "cut off all thoughts."*

My self-deception worked so well that when my grandmother died, three years after our move, the transition seemed subtle; she had only passed from one sector of gone to another. When my mother reported back from the funeral, she said her mother's face had caved in on itself and looked like that of a shrunken witch. I heard my mother say that, but I felt numb.

I told some friends: "my grandma died." Monotonous, composed. Then I had to tell someone in Dutch—an acquaintance, the child of Dutch immigrants, who liked to practise her parents' language with me. *Mijn oma is overleden.*

The pain was immediate and furious. A flood of tears, unstoppable. Early words, along primal neural pathways, imprinted when I still meant everything I said. I never had a grandma, but I had an *oma*.

Years later, I tell my friend Sebastian, "People who speak a language they learned after early childhood live in chronic abstraction."

He says it makes no difference; he feels the same in English or Polish. But one day, when I'm over, his father calls. I hear Sebastian's end of the conversation: younger, faster, and livelier than he sounds in English. It gives me the unsettling sense that I'm friends with a stoic disguise, or more precisely, my disguise is friends with his.

"The second language is an exoskeleton. I often don't feel much in it. Polish is my tender skin," writes Jowita Bydlowska, another linguistic exile.

You can argue, but I heard you, Sebastian. I heard the mazurka of your Polish voice.

piano / piano

The people of the coastal countries of the North Sea used to speak a West Germanic language, or different dialects of West Germanic, somewhat mutually intelligible. When the Romans arrived, unearthing the bedrock and establishing cities, they founded one on the Waal river called Noviomagus, a Celtically derived term for a new market or field, which later became Nijmegen. We biked there in the summers, past orchards, across the Rijn by ferry and the Waal by bridge. That trip was sore thighs and the exhilaration of moving through great open spaces as the city's contours slowly began to loom.

Downtown, I loved the smell inside the oldest churches—an ashen, patchouli damp. We stopped for gelato, which was called *italiaans ijs*. Historically, Dutch is like that; the culturally unknown is given its own descriptive, compound Germanic term. The word raccoon, for example—which is listed in *Webster's Collegiate Dictionary* as arising from "[ärähkun (in some Algonquian language of Virginia)]"—is *wasbeer* in Dutch, or washing-bear, for its habit of moistening its food.

submarine: *under-sea-er*
hospital: *sick-house*
hospitality: *guest-freedom*
thyroid: *shield-gland*
dictionary: *words-book*
ruminant: *re-chewer*
nitrogen: *suffocating-substance*
oxygen: *sour-substance*
concussion: *brain-shaking*
binoculars: *far-lookers*
constellation: *star-image*
anemia: *blood-poverty*
peninsula: *almost*[archaic form]*-island*
protein: *egg-white*
marsupial: *pouch-animal*
liquid: *flowing-substance*

The major linguistic influences on West Germanic include Old Norse, the Latin that the Romans—also people of many dialects—used as their administrative and liturgical language, and the French of later rulers. Germanic scripts had been runic, and were reserved for spiritual ceremony, but the Romans provided a mundane alphabet of the now familiar twenty-six letters. After their rule, the predecessors of modern English, Dutch, and German began to separate.

To speak and write in English from a Dutch background is therefore to have a temporally translucent perspective. Underneath the stream of contemporary English, older words, like river stones, remain in blurred view.

Running water is a living force that refracts, displaces, distorts; sometimes, a sort of sideways drift has taken place among the words, so that the known Dutch term has an English counterpart that no longer means the same thing.

A *penseel,* for instance, is not a pencil, but a paint brush, the kind Vermeer would have used—different from a *kwast,* with which one would paint a house.

A *spreeuw* is not a sparrow, but a starling.

A *tuin* is not a town but a garden.

Lint is ribbon.

A *brief* is a letter, the kind that comes in the mail.

A *stam* is not a stem but a tree trunk.

A *fabriek* is not fabric but a factory.

A *vest* is a cardigan.

A *dier* is an animal.

Afval is not offal, but garbage.

A *blad* is not a blade but a leaf, and also a sheet when referring to paper.

To *huil* is not to howl but to cry.

A *geest* is not so much a ghost as a spirit, and is also used for genie, which English has adapted instead from the Arabic *jinni.*

A *fles* is a bottle, which probably has something to do with a flask. A *rozenbottel* is a rosehip.

And in a very strange confluence, an *eekhoorn,* which is pronounced almost exactly like acorn, is a squirrel.

Boom, a tree. *Tree,* a step of the stairs. Stairs, a *trap*. Trap, a *val*, which also means fall, perhaps because of those archaic traps, holes dug on forest trails and covered with sticks and leaves. The season of fall, *herfst*.

When I write poems, I am still drawn to the Germanic inside the English. There is the familiarity of resemblance—the electric current that runs between my first namings, uttered as a toddler, to the present motions of a pen on the page. Those are the words that retain an immediacy and emotional weight. My poetic vocabulary, then, has something to do with allowing myself to feel the language, or performing Kafka's imperative on myself; that the words are an axe to the frozen sea within me.

I am not alone in favouring the Germanic; in a British study, the one hundred English words in most common daily use in the United Kingdom were all Germanically rooted. English words of Latinate origins remain broadly associated with scholarship, sophistication, and abstraction, whereas Germanic words often register as concrete, blunt, and trusted. My inclination represents an abridged version of a vast, slow process.

In a sense, my poems take the form of spectral piano scores. Dutch is the left hand, the bass clef, but I'm the only one who hears it clearly. English is the melodic right hand, the one that others hear. When my left and right hands are in tune, I am speaking from something deep and elemental, from my grounding, from generations long before me. When the right hand departs and does its own thing, dissonant or incongruous, then I am improvising. I allow myself to drown the left hand out. Then the phrases get conceptual, or playful, or theatrical; on some lucky days, the feeling is that great, unanchored freedom of leaving the ground.

When I write a Dutch poem, that is also my left hand writing, but in a different sense; I feel scrawling and uncoordinated. What has happened would have been unimaginable to me at twelve years old; my Dutch is no longer sure of itself. I write in searching, disoriented trajectories, not in control of the medium. The resulting poems appear primal and strange to me, but the truth is that I don't possess an astute, contemporary idea of how they read. Handwritten and shadowy, taped to my wall, they speak to me as possible omens of English work.

Naturally, despite its relative resistance to influences, Dutch evolves. In recent decades, it has borrowed words with near abandon from English itself. Anglicisms, as the imported words and phrases are called, permeate everyday conversation in the Netherlands, and are abundant on commercial signage and packaging. Among younger people, fragments of English in everyday speech signify worldliness.

These English words, however, are pronounced with distinctly a Dutch slant. Even the ubiquitous term fuck is altered to sound as it reads in Dutch, with its vowel resembling a shortened version of the "ea" in learn. The conjugations of English verbs and pluralization of nouns may also be modified according to Dutch conventions. So the speakers maintain a playful and creative relationship with spoken English; the idea is not to present as an Anglophone, but to maintain the Dutch syntax and sonics. What this means when I visit the Netherlands is that I have the curious option of expressing English terms as I do in Canada, making them sound foreign and occasionally even incomprehensible to family and friends, or adopting what is sometimes called a Dinglish pronunciation, and sounding fraudulent to myself.

On my latest visit, I overheard the following conversation, in Dutch, between two high school students.

Student 1: What are you doing tonight?

Student 2: I don't know. My mom is having people over, but I'm not really looking forward to it because they speak English.

Student 1: Aren't you a star at English, though?

Student 2 (indignant): Yeah, I'm really good at it, but not with "*nay-tiff spiekers!*"

In his virtuosic poem, *mi have een droom (Rotterdam, 2059)*, former Dutch poet laureate Ramsey Nasr writes in a self-invented Dutch of the future. The new tongue has integrated the street language of his city with phrases from Sranantongo, English, Arabic, and German, and gained its own neologisms. The irony is that the speaker delivers a familiar conservative, anti-immigrant rant. What the poem's form also conveys is that the spoken Dutch now taken for granted as standard is already an amalgam, and that the dream or nightmare of a pure culture is as illusory as that of a pure language.

quarantaine / quarantine

Late one afternoon, while reading on the back steps of my home, I overheard a conversation across the far corner of the fence. Two men were talking over beers, in relaxed, accented English, and something drew me to their phrasings—I was hearing familiar intonations, and also a foreign slant. I couldn't decide if their background was French or Dutch or perhaps even German.

A few days later, we were out at the same time again, and I heard the younger man making a phone call. He was speaking Flemish. He wished the person on the line a happy Mother's Day, his voice affectionate and slightly bored. Then he passed the phone to the older man, who turned out to be the mother's brother, and he too wished her well.

Flemish is sometimes called Belgian-Dutch or South-Dutch; it is formally considered a variant of Dutch, and comprises a range of dialects itself. I find it very beautiful to the ear, more lyrical than the northern staccato, almost as if it inflects the Dutch I learned with tenderness. But here I am speaking of the Flemish that I can follow, which often simply means a Flemish person speaking standard Dutch; there are regional variations that would take months of immersion for me to understand. One of my favourite poems is by a Belgian writer, and I always hear the Flemish intonations when I read it on the page:

Poëzie

Zoals je tegen een ziek dochtertje zegt,
mijn miniatuurmensje, mijn zelfgemaakt
verdrietje, en het helpt niet.
Zoals je een hand op haar witte voorhoofd legt,
zo dun als sneeuw gaat liggen,
en het helpt niet.
Zo helpt poezie.

—Herman de Coninck

Poetry

The way you say to a sick little daughter,
my miniature human, my small homemade
sorrow, and it doesn't help.
The way you lay a hand on her white forehead,
as thinly as the snow lays down,
and it doesn't help.
So poetry helps.

After the phone call, I introduced myself over the fence, starting out in English, then switching to Dutch. The older fellow, who had lived in Canada for thirty years, was pleased. "If it wasn't Mother's Day, you never would've heard that! It's the only time in the year that I have a reason to speak Flemish!"

I once took an undergraduate course in ecology. We learned about the life-cycle of *Dicrocoelium dendriticum*, a fluke that on magnification looks like a grain of rice with feathery innards. It lays it eggs in the livers of grazing animals like sheep, and then the eggs move outside via the sheep's manure. Some of them are eaten by snails; these eggs open, and the hatchlings are ejected in mucus globules through the snail's damp skin. The globules are ingested by ants and then the fluke tunnels through the ant's head, and settles in the motor cortex of its brain. In daylight, the infected ant continues to behave as if nothing is wrong, but after sundown, it feels driven to crawl up to a grass blade's tip, and to clench the grass in its jaws, holding on until morning. The ant does so nightly, until it is eaten by a grazing sheep. Then the fluke's cycle starts again.

The sound of the Flemish accents in the backyard held a strange power over me. On numerous subsequent evenings, I climbed the back stairs and sat on the top step to listen. It was only the imprint of Flemish within English; still, there was a compulsion—in the atmosphere of that accent, the mild spring nights seemed to release their stubborn anchoring in the present. Perhaps the language in my cortex has a homing instinct, wanting to be positioned where it might be swallowed back into the whole, the auditory cosmos of its origins.

raadsel / riddle

I was in a doctor's office in Toronto when I saw a display rack that offered the same flyer on breast self-examination in at least twelve different languages. I took one—I couldn't read the script, but it was so beautiful; there was an intrinsic continuity, a horizontal line from which stark, clear letters hung suspended. I taped it to the wall over my desk. Months later, I found out that it was my father's mother tongue; Punjabi, the language of the land of five waters or rivers, where I had never been.

There are two Punjabi scripts. The flyer was in Gurmukhi, which means "from the guru's mouth." Shahmukhi, "from the king's mouth," has a wispier, curvilinear alphabet. The two forms of writing denote the same spoken language, but they are not similar; they're written in opposite directions, and a reader of one cannot automatically read the other. Although the two scripts long precede the colonial partition of India and Pakistan, their use has taken on political implications, so that now Gurmukhi is generally the Indian form of Punjabi writing, and Shahmukhi is Pakistani.

My father told me recently that he had no idea, when he left Kenya, that he would start to forget his first language. He was worried about whether or not he would be able to speak enough Punjabi during an upcoming visit with his family. Then he translated a Punjabi saying for me: "Lose your wealth, lose a little. Lose your health, lose a lot. Lose your language, lose everything."

"What do you think it means?" I asked "Is it about identity?"

"Identity…" he affirmed, "But also, it tells you their history. Anyone who came up with that saying must have lost their language at some point."

My father's linguistic state is an example of what Yildiz describes in *Beyond The Mother Tongue: The Post-Monolingual Condition*; he does not have a single first language, and learned Punjabi, Urdu, English, and Swahili almost simultaneously. As an adult, fluency in Dutch followed. Still, when I ask him what he considers to be his mother tongue, he doesn't hesitate to say Punjabi.

For the year or so that we lived in Kenya while I was a pre-schooler, I had a small vocabulary in his languages. What remains are funny fragments. In Swahili, I can count to seven, exchange a greeting, and name a lion, a giraffe, a cooking pot. In Punjabi or Urdu, I can tell a child to be quiet. I know the parts of the outfits I would have worn at Eid; the *salwar kamiz*, the *chuni* shawl, the *mehndi* on my hands. From later years, I can repeat the listening affirmations that someone might make on the phone. An array of kitchen words are still in use in my parents' home: *dhania* for cilantro, *atta* for flour, *haldi* for turmeric.

The reasons that I do not speak my father's languages become more circular in causation the more I consider them. I didn't live in his country for long. He didn't speak Punjabi to us. We weren't close while I still lived at home. And his languages held no promise in a racist culture. Even his kind of English, tempered with a South Asian melodiousness, was considered comedic on television, while my mother's Dutch accent never seemed to be inherently funny.

Over the years, I've made small attempts at contact with Punjabi. In the folder of drawings and writings that my mother saved from my grade school years, there's a scrap of paper with my phonetic and pictorial translations of a few words: shoe, arm, shirt, and head. I must have asked my father to teach me. I've taken out a book from the library and mouthed the words. A few years ago, I approached the teenager whose family owned a small grocery store nearby, to ask if someone there would be willing to give me lessons. He looked me over and tried to dissuade me: "You don't want to learn Punjabi," he said, "it's only a village language. And it's really fast, like rap. You should learn Urdu, which is more beautiful. Then you can read poetry."

My father and I are driving down a highway edged with cornfields and sprawl, small cedars hugging the slope of overpasses, manufacturing plants perforated with truck docks, all under an enormous sky of cumulus and blue. The scene has the cheerful serenity of Jack Chambers' painting *401 Towards London*, the inspiration for which came when Chambers looked in his rear-view mirror while driving to Toronto. We're going the same way, to the city that first received us long ago, and where I still love to eavesdrop, listening for the linguistic currents and drifts within families: Greek curses within an otherwise English conversation, multi-lingual children translating for their parents, the assertive intonations of Arabic. Since our migration, my father and I have become accustomed to speaking English to each other. Dutch is for private subjects that arise in public: money, or strained relations, or ailments.

Our relationship is mending. He is the only person I know who loves certain works of Dutch fiction for the same reasons that I do. He gives me *Het Bureau* and *Nooit Meer Slapen,* books whose sentences embody what James Baldwin called for from writers; they are as clean as a bone.

Jagjit Singh's ghazals are playing on the tape deck, in Urdu or Punjabi—I can't tell. "What's he singing right now?" I ask.

My father sounds slightly embarrassed: "Oh, it is all very flowery, very melodramatic. He's singing: 'This journey is not of our making. We go in whichever direction the wind blows. With time, the journey of the sands has lasted eons.' That's the style."

We smile. He knows that I'm used to the sober, concise wordings of Dutch, and the slightly more elliptical but still emotionally flattened phrases of English. Quietly, I hold on to Singh's lines that contain so much of the immaterial—even the concrete nouns of wind and sand are vast and only partly substantial.

The culture of the Netherlands raised me to accept logic as the means to truth, and to waste nothing; not bread, or clothes, or words. When used as in "that's such a waste," the Dutch word is the same as the one for sin. Moderation in aesthetics and emotions were, in the Calvinist tradition, considered virtuous. I had understood this well enough, but never entirely comfortably. My oldest uncle, a kind and meticulous northerner, once wrote to us of a family funeral. He described the line of relations who had paid their last respects at the grave with a nod to the lowered coffin. Then, he wrote, it was the turn of my cousin's wife, a woman from a southern province; she blew a kiss and tossed a rose. He was moved by her gesture, which he attributed to the different cultures of the regions. When I read that, I wanted to be from the south.

What a strangely relative South that was; perhaps a hundred kilometers away, somewhat less coastal than the North, its temperatures a degree or two above our own—but the people were generally Catholic, which meant indulgent of power and beauty.

I have thought about Punjabi in practical, Dutch terms; as a means to speak and listen to my grandmother, aunts, uncles, and cousins. Now, in a car on the 401, I wonder for the first time how I myself would have translated in that flowery village language—whether the territory of my inner life, the parts I allowed for and the ones I suppressed, might have been a different country.

stilte / silence

castle	*kasteel*
river	*rivier*
fabric	*fabriek* (factory)
palace	*paleis*
ocean	*oceaan*
quarter	*kwartier*
furnace	*fornuis* (stove)
curtain	*gordijn*
carpet	*tapijt*
jewel	*juweel*
formal	*formeel*
pheasant	*fazant*
paper	*papier*
fountain	*fontein*
accent	*accent*
traffic	*verkeer*
rabbit	*konijn*

In English, the words on this list are pronounced as trochees, with weight placed on the first sylla-ble, while in Dutch they are iambs, in which the second syllable is emphasized. In both languages, the emphasis is generally accomplished by the full pronunciation of the vowel, a slight elongation of the syllable, and a subtle increase in its volume and pitch, although the element of pitch also depends on whether a question is being asked.

A trochee is the sound of something landing after a fall; an initial thud, followed by a smaller bounce. An apple from a tree. It is a passive, downhill sound, entropic and relinquishing. In iambs, the first syllable is a prelude, or a warning; something is about to happen, and then it does. An iamb is an effort of the will.

In both languages, we consider the heartbeat to be iambic, lub-<u>dub</u>. This means the iambic pentameter of Shakespeare's plays and sonnets are like a pulse—although the English physician William Harvey, who was his contemporary, and described the heart sounds in some detail, only compared them to the gulping sound made by a horse drinking water.

Words are small gestures, their structures expressive, and so a river is not a *rivier*. A river, in its diminishing sounds, is the sight of a silver ribbon of water, turning and narrowing toward a horizon. A *rivier* is the water's proximal presence; the shore's waves washing over your rubber boots.

Martinus Nijhoff, in his iconic 1934 long poem *Awater*—a work that Joseph Brodsky called one of the grandest of the twentieth century—used iambic pentameter, as well as a pattern of assonant end-rhymes. The latter has so far proven impossible to translate into English. Nijhoff's opening lines are an invocation:

Wees hier aanwezig, allereerste geest,
die over wateren van aanvang zweeft.

Literally, and in their Dutch order, the words translate something like this:

Be here present, very-first spirit,
that over waters of commencement floats.

"Spirit" is closest in meaning, but in terms of rhyme and aligning words of the same Germanic origin, "ghost" would be more appropriate.

Daan van der Vat, a Dutch journalist and acclaimed writer of nonsense verse, produced the first English translation of *Awater* in 1949. He worked in consultation with Nijhoff, and his opening lines are:

Primordial Ghost, Spirit of Genesis,
Haunting the waters of earth's infancy,

In 1961, James S. Holmes published a new translation that starts as follows:

Be present here, spirit primordial
that hovers over waters of beginning.

David Colmer, in 2010, begins like this:

Be here with me, immortal timeless being,
that moves upon the face of nascent waters.

The three translations, in their divergent incarnations of the poem, are instructive in the possibilities and limits of movements from Dutch to English.

When comparing, van der Vat's two lines use more illustrious diction than the original. He also does not end-stop the second line, partly because he doesn't directly call for the spirit's presence until the third line. What he says then, "abide with me," has a diluted effect because of its delayed occurrence, and its relative formality.

As a correspondent for a Dutch newspaper, van der Vat lived in London for many years, and was married to a British woman; he was fluent in English, but his translation of *Awater* as a whole suggests that he may not have possessed a native speaker's comfort with the casual register of the language. Or perhaps his wish to have his friend's poem received with respect and admiration in the English world caused him to stray from its simple vocabulary to a more erudite one. His capitalization of each line contributes further to the sense that he wished to establish the work's canonical importance. Unfortunately, these techniques seem to inadvertently betray some of the poem's foundational strengths, which are its clear and accessible language, and its natural phrasing.

The original poem's notion of a "very-first spirit" is inherently primordial—van der Vat begins to describe rather than represent this, and produces a more explicitly biblical image, which narrows the eternal invocation to a limited, historical context.

Nijhoff, however, was pleased with the translation; in one of his letters to his friend, he comments on a line in the poem and notes: "yours is better than the Dutch!" He recognized, rightly, that van der Vat had taken on and completed an almost impossible task; and so the first version of *Awater* crossed the North Sea.

In Holmes' rendition of *Awater*, the opening lines have a closer kinship with the original; they have been rendered with simplicity, and there is no artificial capitalization. This fidelity seems like the obvious route, but Holmes was probably more able to follow it because his predecessor's version had already generated real international interest in Nijhoff's work; Holmes did not need to convince an editor of the poem's significance. Another advantage for Holmes was that *Awater* was now definitively complete, whereas van der Vat had worked with a poem that was still being altered by its writer. And Holmes had an existing English text to work with, along with the Dutch original; he could take or leave material from van der Vat's example as he worked.

Awater's structure was based on the ancient French poem, *Song of Roland*. Holmes admired Nijhoff's reproduction of this older form, and studied its particulars. As his first lines suggest, he was able to reiterate its metric qualities, including a pentameter that often features a stressed fourth syllable. Holmes acknowledged that "short of writing a new poem," he saw no way to reproduce the vowel-based rhymes of the original.

"Primordial," as used by Holmes, remains a more explanatory, academic term than "very-first," but of course there is no English word that will substitute directly for the Dutch compound term, which almost amounts to "*first*est." With "hovers," his translation comes closest to the Dutch word "zweeft." I denoted it as "floats" for the sake of the single syllable ending with a *t*, and a potential evocation of the rhyme with "ghost"—but technically, "zweeft" refers only to a suspension in air, not water, so that "hovers" is more accurate. Whatever the verb, there is no natural English grammar that positions it at the end of the line as in Dutch, so that the couplet can't end on that same soft, mysterious aspect of the image. Importantly, however, the potent first word of the poem, "Be," is reproduced by Holmes in its place. Elsewhere in the translation, his attention to phrasing allows him to restore crucial elements of meaning, such as the speaker's mother being dead, a line that van der Vat's more verbose approach had caused him to omit for lack of space.

Colmer, in *Awater*'s most recent translation, reproduces not only the poem's first word, but its first two, "Be here," which accomplishes, both in consonant and vowel sounds and in syllabic stress, a close sonic echo of the Dutch. It occurs at the essential, germinal moment. The compromise is that this word order precludes the term "present," so that Colmer has to insert a "me,"—a self-reference that the original does not get around to until the fourteenth line, which opens the second stanza. In this, some of the breadth of the first section is lost, and perhaps that is why he reinvokes it in the words that follow—"immortal, timeless being."

Colmer's second line restores a shade of the formality that Holmes left behind—"upon" instead of "over," "nascent" rather than "beginning." However, it is a line that is metrically accurate and has a beautiful, appropriately incantatory sound. Colmer has recreated, as the first two translators could not, some of the assonant rhyme of *Awater*; like Holmes, he admits that he saw no means to reproduce Nijhoff's end-rhymes in the English version, but he has incorporated internal rhymes and resonances—here/me/being, face/nascent, immortal/waters—that acknowledge the original poem's music. *Awater* is a compelling pleasure to read out loud, and Colmer's translation is the one that preserves that elemental characteristic.

Iambic pentameter—a pulse, a horse at a trough—when translated between Dutch and English, requires creative adjustments. This is evident later on in *Awater*, where terminal words like soldier, metal and office (sol<u>daat</u>, me<u>taal</u>, kan<u>toor</u>) are—in Colmer's example—either shuffled back within their lines, or traded, in a sense; allowed to remain in position, while an adjacent line that ends on a trochee is made iambic, so that the prevailing rhythm is preserved.

When we absorb images, dance or music from a culture outside our own, we may project substantial misinterpretations, but it is also possible to receive the sense of what was intended: a face, a fright, an ode. A written poem in a foreign language is inscrutable. Someone has to ferry it across the difference. The three published English versions of *Awater* illustrate that a translator's perception of what is essential to the original work, the context of their translation process, and their skills, make every version its own creature. To translate a poem faithfully is to balance an algebra not made to be solved; a task for which it does not hurt to invoke the primordial spirits.

tijd / time

"What makes photography a strange invention is that its primary raw materials are light and time," John Berger wrote.

In the Dutch city of Tilburg, Ria van Dijk has made an annual visit to the shooting tent of the *kermis*, the traveling fair, for more than three quarters of a century. With unfailing aim, she has fired the air rifle, and activated a mounted camera that takes a portrait of her and whomever else is inside the frame.

Part of what makes her series of pictures so compelling is its compression of time. Van Dijk ages from a self-assured teenager into a robust, cheerful grandmother figure, and the bystanders' appearances change—at first they wear proper suits and hats, but their garments shift with each decade, culminating in relaxed, contemporary streetwear. At some point, colour is introduced, with an almost profane effect, and in a later picture, a group of journalists surrounds van Dijk. English words appear increasingly in the background signs: big, palace, hug.

Still, time is not uniformly progressive in the photographs. Van Dijk only changes slowly, with her reliably short, waved hairstyle, her steady posture and confident gaze, while around her the world seems to turn over at a different speed. And of course the shooting tent itself is a constant—first a novelty and then a relic, but preserved. There is something of the suicidal in her gesture, even though she is shooting a target, not a mirror; something of the miraculous in her perpetual reappearance, her survival of the shot.

Photography, of course, employs that shooting language, although its usage is more common in English than in Dutch. In English we take a picture, which seems to relate the activity to its subject, while in Dutch it is more usual to make one, drawing attention to the photographer's effort. English speakers "are in the picture"—they happen to be in the frame—but Dutch ones "stand on the photo;" they are choosing to be included.

I grew up calling a camera a *fototoestel*, a photo-device, but when I went to the Netherlands more recently, I heard a few people say *camera*. I wondered who would be more likely to use one term or the other; whether it depended on the speaker's age, or if they also spoke English, or owned a television or computer, or were rural or urban dwellers—because time has such local and private velocities.

At our first Canadian school, a black and white picture of each new student was taped to the "Welcome Wall" outside the office. I don't remember the photos being taken, but I can still see my youngest brother's impish smile, the middle one's missing front tooth, and my own hair hastily pinned to one side. That was us, at the start of our English education. It's not that our Dutch arrested there; after that flash of light, we still used our language at home, and on return visits—but the era of continuous immersion was over, and the effect was immediate enough that even now, when we speak Dutch, the imprint of our ages in the photographs remains. In my youngest brother's voice, the intonations of early childhood are audible. In my middle brother's mind, the words for foods he loved as a boy remain easily recalled: black currant soda, paprika-flavoured chips, cheese buns. He can elaborate on the comic strips *Asterix and Obelix,* and *Suske and Wiske*, but has a harder time explaining what he does for a living.

I still think of myself as fluent, but I have almost no medical or financial vocabulary, and when those subjects arise, I resort to circuitous descriptions: the gland that regulates blood sugar levels, the taxes paid for owning a house. I've forgotten the written grammatical particulars that I learned in the last years before our departure, and I'm in doubt, when I write a letter, whether to end conjugations of certain verbs with a d or a t, or both. In conversation, I can sound amusingly formal—"like a book," said one friend— and it's true that unless I'm in the Netherlands, Dutch is primarily a reading language to me now. The skill of casual exchanges is in gradual atrophy.

You shoot yourself and live. Is that what happens when you switch languages?

In *Nederland*, my mother was mostly at home, and it was a very social place; the front door was unlocked, and friends or relatives came and went often, and sometimes stayed for weeks. Many loved my father's cooking. He taught them the skill of scooping a bite of curry with a torn piece of roti. Their houses welcomed us as well. There were evenings when my brothers and I would cycle between places, surveying what was for dinner, and then choose where to eat.

In retrospect, I know how much our family needed that fabric of relations. It meant that our home lives were witnessed, and there were other places to spend an afternoon or a few days, so that our struggles never outgrew our capacities; they found integration and balance in the presence of friends and relatives.

In Canada, our house became more of a closed capsule, a calcification around the tumult of our adjustments. At first, my mother was at home, watching television to practice Canadian English and numb her loneliness, or she was doing the work that was available, because her degrees wouldn't be acknowledged until years later; she looked after other children or cleaned houses. We joined her once, on a day when there was no school, in the most silent apartment I have ever known—my brothers pushed toy cars around while I polished the legs of wooden chairs and saw my mother tighten her smile around a quiet anger.

Slowly, the narrative that she tried so fervently to uphold in front of others—that our new lives were joyful and successful, that everything was going well—started to feel poisonous to me. I did not want to misuse words like that; I didn't want to summon them into a performance that would distort our relations.

At the same time, I held great admiration for her. My mother became a supply teacher, and by then, the responsibility of earning for our family had come to rest on her shoulders. She worked incredibly hard in a language that never became entirely comfortable for her. Later, when she had her own classroom, I would help prepare materials, or edit her report cards. My mother was frugal in a manner that made many things possible for us. I don't think she ever even bought herself a cup of coffee outside the house; I, on the other hand, had weekly violin lessons. That was the form her love took.

My compromise was to be silent in person—I got used to standing quietly beside her as she regaled people with our invented or exaggerated accomplishments—and to make furtive attempts at truthfulness on paper, in notebooks housed far under my bed. It was there, in poems, that I wrote of feeling suicidal and lonely. My mother would not hear me out on those subjects; it was as if the less I resembled the stories she told, the less she wanted to know me.

As a teacher, my mother also had an annual picture taken. It would come in a paper frame along with the group portrait of her Special Education class, eight or nine students who were usually with her for several years. The school was in a part of town where many families lived in poverty. Her smile would be shy, her outfit chosen with concern for the British formality that she associated with the new culture. The children around her looked happy; they trusted her, a feeling that did not depend on her English. When I see her pictures now, I still feel the ache of those years, but there is a medicinal element in recognizing that other children, some of whom had very little to rely on in their lives, received her attention in my stead.

These days, my mother is the steadiest source of Dutch conversation in my life. Even her fluid, lucid, and enthusiastic Dutch is subtly evolving. English words, more readily at hand, are swapped in here and there in her speech and in mine—a habit we used to notice among older Dutch immigrants, and imagined ourselves immune to. At other moments, we both falter and have to remind each other of the Dutch word we're looking for; it is a sensation familiar to dreams, to be certain that something exists without being able to locate it.

Irrationally, I want her Dutch to be constant and enduring—perhaps it represents her earliest presence to me, the mother who created a household full of voices. I wonder what it will be like for her to age in this country, and to come to rest in soil so far from her origins. Our mutual history is clouded with pain, but sometimes, lately, I feel the fog clear; I understand that she gave me what she could. And when I consider what I can give her now, the first thing that comes to mind is that I can speak and listen in Dutch if she needs it. She navigated our immigration with a proverb in mind: "Of the concert of life, no one gets a program," but thirty years later it is Ovid's phrase from *Metamorphoses* that I hold onto: "Everything changes, nothing is lost."

uier / udder

A neighbour down the street introduced himself one day as I walked past his family's house. He was perhaps the same age as my parents. His light blue eyes had friendly contours, and his hands were stained with grease from working on an engine. His accent sounded Dutch. I asked, and then said that I was Dutch too, and watched him closely.

I have come to love and respect each strand of my background, and if I feel the need to make the declaration, then I usually call myself mixed, or specify that I'm Dutch-Kenyan-Pakistani-Afghani. But when I meet a white Dutch person, I often say Dutch. The gesture always feels quietly precipitous—it is, of course, a litmus test of a person's perspective; is their *Nederland* the vibrant cultural amalgam that is my birthplace, or do they cling to racist notions of who belongs? Not only will their answer settle that, it will determine what remains possible between us.

If they flinch, if their brow creases in, if they say, "but you," etcetera, then I may still be their acquaintance or colleague or neighbour, but a boundary is established; in their view, it is part of the world's inherent order, but I know that they have newly redrawn it, around the small and frightened territory of their self.

My neighbour's face registered only friendliness. He started telling me of his childhood in Friesland. He had been apprenticing at milking cows, early in the morning and again after school. I'd read about that mid-20th-century village life; how the fields progressed through spring and summer tides of wildflowers then, instead of the perpetually green, short grass that defines the rural Netherlands now. I knew that those flowers flavoured the butter; that the herds were small enough for the cows to have names.

We'd both been twelve when we emigrated. We spoke that number and there was a silence. We were of different generations, but momentarily twelve years old, standing on the street where we lived and not seeing it, staring at memories of our departures. I think our friendship may have formed in that gap.

Filmmaker Lester Alfonso made a documentary called *Twelve*, in which he records the experiences of people who, like himself, arrived in Canada at that age. Twelve can be a difficult life stage for migration because the loss of childhood coincides with the loss of home, and our own culture's methods of navigating adolescence may not seem relevant in the new place. Alfonso likens the feeling to being dropped by one's parents at the edge of the woods and having to find the way through alone.

In my own case, I remember the abrupt and immense decline in my independence. At home, my friends and I had our bikes—we could take them to each other's houses, the woods, the movies—and we were in high school, already choosing our areas of study; in Canada, I was suddenly in a school with a kindergarten, and our suburban townhouse meant that I had ask for a ride to get anywhere. For the first time, as well, I was among students who disparaged an enthusiasm for academics, and I learned the untranslatable word "nerd." It was striking, decades later, to watch Alfonso's film and recognize my common ground with the people whom he interviews. I saw them struggle with the residue of a disrupted human process, a maturation that had taken place far from their communities. There was often no discernable accent to their Canadian English; when it came to language, they too wore their origins somewhere within.

My neighbour and I did not need to explain ourselves to each other; we were two people who had been through the woods, and in the evidence of his life—his crowd of children and grandchildren, his history on our street, and love for road trips across Canada—I saw how home takes shape again.

It was he who told me that the red forms on the Friesian flag, which I had written of as hearts, were actually lily pad leaves, *waterleliebladeren* in Dutch, and *pompeblêden* in his province's language.

One of my grandmothers was from Friesland, but lived in a city of metal refineries on the Dutch west coast. I often stayed with her. The people of IJmuiden had their own distinct, working class accent, which seemed casual and loud; the sound of words made to overcome perpetual noise, which in my mind was industrial, though of course their way of speaking was much older than the smelters and the freighters. The drowning out was from the waves and wind; perhaps their "flat" was not of the pastures, as in my own region, but of the flounder served from roadside trucks, and the expanse of the water. I liked the city's people. Though many of them turned tight-lipped when encountering the pair of us—the Friesian woman whom they had always known to live alone, and the foreign-looking girl in her charge—not everyone did, and IJmuidenaren were people of the sea; their stories were generous, unnerving, and never seemed less than true.

Every few evenings, Beppe would pull a chair up the rotary phone in her apartment and dial her sisters, who still resided in the villages of their birth region. I'd hear her speak Friesian, which sounded ancient and rural to me, and seemed foreign to her window's view of apartment lights, distant mounds of ore, and smokestacks topped with blue flames; her voice was mellow and sincere.

"Could you understand?" she'd ask me afterwards, grinning, but a few words or phrases were all I could repeat, even though there seemed to be an intrinsic slowness to the language. It was as if it was all in a lower gear than Dutch, but still too fast to decipher.

Then, as a teenager on return visits to the Netherlands, my comprehension shifted; I could make out whole sentences or segments of conversation. I know now that the difference was English—Friesian is like an old Germanic bridge that connects Dutch to English. There's a rhyme that is used to illustrate the kinship, because it is pronounced similarly in both languages: "butter, bread and green cheese is good English and good Friesian" (West Friesian: *bûter, brea en griene tsiis is goed Ingelsk en goed Frysk*). Curiously, leaving Beppe and learning the colonial language of a country across the Atlantic had brought me closer to her *moedertaal*.

verzen / verses

Nederlands contains few instances of silent letters. When they occur, they are likely to be derived from the French, as in *plafond* (ceiling), or the result of shortened older word forms, as in *erwt* (pea, from *erweete*). In a word such as "half," Dutch calls for the pronunciation of each consonant, hull-f; a knot is a *knoop*, k-nope; light is *licht,* li-[guttural g]-t. To me, the landscape reflects this absence of silent letters, particularly in the west; between the expertly planned railways, highways, bicycle and pedestrian paths, canals and drainage creeks, neighbourhoods, and business parks, a superfluous space has no part in the terrestrial vocabulary.

Spelling and pronunciation are generally governed by logic in Dutch. An Anglophone who memorizes the Dutch alphabet could read a *Nederlands* book out loud and be understood. The word for language itself invokes that logical basis; according to several etymological sources, *taal* comes from the same root as tally, and had to do with counting by notching a stick. A language, from the Latin *lingua*, on the other hand, is of the tongue—and every student of English is familiar with its inconsistencies. As a child, I found reading out loud treacherous and perplexing. The vagaries of English pronunciation may have arisen from intriguing, concurrent regional histories, but at my low desk in an overheated Scarborough portable, they struck me as unfair tricks. How could o-u-g-h sound like tough and cough and through and though and thought and plough? How did the cycle in bicycle turn to sickle? Surely no one could defend a system where no was no, but do was do, and where the locals never enunciated clearly enough to distinguish if their do might actually be dew or due. I finally confronted my teacher over the X in my spelling book beside the word union; in the dictation, he had said onion. I argued my case while he remained amused and apologetic, repeating that the "o" was counterintuitive but nevertheless correct.

English was both a dominant and an eccentric language; no wonder that it had been adapted and interpreted by various groups to make its own local sense. Even in the culture of three that comprised my brothers and I, we improvised on its strangeness, usually while we played with LEGO in our basement. In that shelter of concrete walls and floors, among the hanging laundry and thick rugs, we could discuss if *O Canada* really contained both the French and the Dutch words for chicken, which is what all three of us heard, and we could laugh about words that sounded ridiculous to us, like Connecticut. We tried out cinematic English dialogue between the plastic humans, and attempted the difficult sound of the "h" in huge. Some of our misinterpretations became unwieldy. For example, I implored my brothers to take seriously the signs in our area that said "no trespassing"—I was afraid because not only did our grim Vice Principal pray against trespassing on the school P.A. System, but some of the fences in the neighbourhood said "trespassers will be prosecuted," which I thought meant killed.

At the end of grade 6, as we prepared to return to the Netherlands, my teachers gave me a thesaurus. I still love that book; it's been so well used that many of the black, half-moon labels of the thumb index have fallen out. I'm fascinated by the possibilities that fracture prismatically from each starting term. I had never heard of a thesaurus in Dutch, but the book with the dinosaur name made intuitive sense; English had always felt bigger. There may be no numerical basis for that perception; the latest edition of the *Oxford English Dictionary* defines 171,476 terms, while the current *van Dale*, the Dutch standard, specifies approximately 240,000 words. But vocabularies are very difficult to quantify—there is the consideration of contemporary versus archaic terms, the inclusion of variations and scientific jargon, and the prevalence of compound words. The latter are in generous use in *Nederlands*; kitchenchair, leadpoisoning, powderedsugar, and coldwaterfear are all, in translation, regular Dutch words. The practice of stringing words together into legitimate single terms inflates Dutch dictionaries to some degree. At the same time, English may feel larger to me not through its actual vocabulary but because of the enormous number of people who speak it, its vast geographic territory, and its prevalence in popular culture.

Poetry was in my life from an early age. I loved the work of Annie M.G. Schmidt, whose poetry and stories were inseparable from Dutch childhoods of my generation. Her poems were expertly metered and rhymed, funny and sardonic, and they often centralized the child's voice. Poems were also the traditional accompaniment to *Sinterklaasavond*— St. Nicholas' evening; a verse was offered along with each present. In our family, we also wrote poetry for birthdays and anniversaries. My Opa excelled at this quaint art form—he sent me poems even on occasions such as an ice storm, and getting my hair cut short.

This sort of playful writing, with its prescribed forms, was an activity I could resume fairly soon in English. I wrote my first English poem in E.S.L. class at Halloween and I still have it; it was about a witch who accidentally took her own potion. "She put some brew, by mistake,/ in her witch's spider cake./ And when she had her cake for lunch,/ you heard a thunder and a crunch,/ you heard a scream and a howl,/ the witch had changed into an owl." Mrs. Turnpenny advised me to change each "you heard" to "there was," but I still coveted to old

130

Dutch syntax ("heard you"), though I had learned to invert it.

It took much longer for me to start hearing the subtle qualities of English. Often, its sounds remained slack and glutinous to my ear, undistinguished, a muddied stream. For years into adolescence, the only poems that spoke to my fierce maelstroms of feeling were in Dutch. Eventually, though, English poems started to appear on my bedroom wall. What had sounded atonal and awkward was very slowly taking on hushed musical registers, and then, at last, the language sang. There was *The Flower-fed Buffaloes of the Spring*, by Lindsay Vachel—in which I only later recognized the myth of Indigenous extinction, "the Blackfoot, lying low, the Pawnees, lying low,"—and *Preface to a Twenty-Volume Suicide Note,* by Amiri Baraka. I don't remember where I found them. I was in love with the cadences and the melancholy of Vachel's poem, and the manner in which Baraka's lines sprawled, and then paused in that potently slowing line, "things have come to that." English, to me, had begun to have wide, uneven possibilities; room for the exploratory, tripping movements of a phrase.

Ten years after I heard Leo Vroman read, I learned that Baraka would be reading at the campus in Kingston, where I lived. Again, I had the sense of being drawn into an event that could change me. He read in a crammed auditorium, and his delivery was nothing like Vroman's murmuring; his voice resounded in the stained glass windows, in the follicles of my hair. I didn't feel comforted or nostalgic; I felt enlivened and summoned. Afterwards, at the book-signing table, he invited me to give him some poems, and he later sent me an encouraging postcard. Emerging into that summer night, having given him a scavenged peony, I knew I could retune to an English register.

waarschuwing / warning

One afternoon, well into my Canadian life, I was riding my bike through a downtown intersection. On the opposite corner, a cluster of pedestrians waited to cross. Something large was on the road in front of them, against the gutter, blocking my path. A garbage bag. I swerved left to avoid it, and a young man in the small crowd yelled *"Pas op!"* I looked over my left shoulder and saw that I'd moved in front of a speeding pickup truck, and when I swung back to the edge of the street, it barrelled through and I felt the airstream as its side mirror passed my head.

I was already a few blocks away, feeling foolish, lucky, and shaken, when I realized I'd been alerted in Dutch. Maybe by a tourist, or an exchange student, who in a moment of alarm had spewed the first words that came to mind. For which I happened to be wired, as it were, from ears to brain to palms gripping the ribbed handlebars.

Mother tongue, is this how you come to your estranged ones, in wayward outbursts, sparing their lives?

Not long ago, a child named Nancy was interned at the Kamloops Indian Residential School. She was forgetting parts of her language. Not through the slow attrition of immigration, but from the purposeful brutality of her teachers, and of their supervisors, and of their supervisors' supervisors, in a funnel of power under which a young girl, stolen from her parents, was a lonesome target. She recalls lying in bed one evening: "I remembered trying to remember some words... I was trying to remember one word and that was *squirrel* and it was so easy... I remember struggling with it all day and trying to remember. And then at night when I went to bed, I kept thinking about it and thought and thought and then it came up—*dlig*."

Mother tongue, is this when you'll surface, under cover of night, in the mind's somnolent dark?

I once worked on a hospital ward where an elderly woman lay in a catatonic state. She stayed in bed, refused to drink, eat, or speak, and kept her eyes fixed on the ceiling. Because there was nothing measurably wrong, the medical doctors had been confounded and transferred her to psychiatry. There was no known family. The nurses turned her stiff body in the bed. Sometimes they managed to feed her a spoonful of water or soup.

The woman had been brought to the hospital by her landlord, who described her as determined and self-reliant, a widowed Dutch immigrant. He said she didn't answer her door for a day or two, and he found her sitting mute and immobile in a chair. I could picture that chair. Upholstered in dim florals, brown crocheted covers over the arm rests. The carpet still scrolled with a vacuum's linear wake. The tick of a heavy, wooden clock.

I offered to speak Dutch to her. The staff agreed, and they gathered around her bed to observe. I stood beside the IV pole with its translucent bag of fluid and the nightstand where a small pink sponge on a stick sat in a Styrofoam cup of water. The woman was emaciated, her body dry as kindling under the sheets. I had the sense that a formidable will was at work. Perhaps she had made up her mind to die. I asked, in Dutch, *"Mrs. P, can we do anything for you?"*

The effect was abrupt. She snapped her head sideways and searched out my eyes in the group. Her gaze was bewildered, imploring, and furious. Holding it made me tremble. Then, only once, she shook her head conclusively. Turning away, she resumed her petrified state.

Mother tongue, will you come for your uprooted ones, when our souring, laboured breaths are numbered? Will you be there to ferry us home?

xenofobie / xenophobia

Dutch words that do not exist in English include *leeshonger* (a hunger to read), *afbellen* (to cancel plans by phone), and *gezellig*. The latter is sometimes translated as "cozy," but it is possible to be cozy in solitude, while *gezellig*, which shares its root with the Dutch word for companionship, usually describes a relaxed and enjoyable social atmosphere, or a space that invites a gathering. It's also possible to be *ongezellig*; to fail to be cheerful in the context of a jovial group.

Other expressions translate poorly because they refer to particular places. My favourite is *voor Pampus liggen,* to "lie before Pampus," which refers to a sandbank in the waters off Amsterdam. Large ships that reached Pampus at low tide used to have to wait until the water rose before they could enter the harbour; to say that you are lying before Pampus is to declare yourself idle and recumbent—it could be for pleasure, from exhaustion, or from excess food or drink. The *Mokerheide* is a specific heath, but also means as far away as possible. *Bij Neck* (an isolated village) *om naar* (around to) *Den Haag* (the Hague) is to take an unnecessarily circuitous route.

I have not experienced the limits of my languages as the limits of my world, but I am familiar with the sweet revelation of finding that the formerly inexpressible has a name.

A friend of mine loves to be out on blustery days; a part of her has long intuited the clarifying nature of the wind's force. When I told her of the Dutch term *uitwaaien*, which means to take a walk in strong winds in order to refresh oneself, I was naming a concept that already lived in her; hearing the word was an affirmation.

This happened for me when I learned the Punjabi word *jugaad*. I'd been aware that my father had an unusually makeshift approach to materials. He picked things up from the curb on garbage day and repaired them. He made shelves out of the packing containers of our move. Recently, at my parents' home, I saw that he had fashioned a baby gate for the grandchildren out of a bed's headboard and two rubber exercise bands. As a teenager, my response to his contraptions used to take the form of an inner dispute; I felt embarrassment at their oddness, and also pride in what I took to be a hold-over from Kenyan culture, where children made soccer balls out of elastics, and toy cars out of tin cans (there is a Swahili term for this inventiveness as well; *jua kali*). Now I thoroughly appreciate them as frugal, unpretentious and self-sufficient. Unlike the sanctioned alternative—the immediate purchase of a designated and eventually disposable product—their construction is a creative process, and does no further ecological harm. I seem to have inherited the practice; my standing desk, for example, has long been a cardboard box on a table, and I've used the silver lids of take-out containers to reflect light onto houseplants. These wayward solutions are *jugaad*; they make do with what is at hand. Although I was alone when I learned the term, a sense of community arrived with it; I'd tried to describe the spirit of *jugaad* to a few friends, but it turned out there were millions of people who already understood.

To name experience is a clarifying sensation; it is more mysterious to find that there are words for what we may never have considered. For me, this was true when I read *The Spirit Catches You And You Fall Down*, where Anne Fadiman lists the meanings of a number of Hmong expressions, including *txij txej* (a rat or mouse crying out in a snake's mouth) and *nqaj nqug* (many trees falling, one right after another). Soraya Peerbaye writes in her collection *Poems for the Advisory Committee on Antarctic Names* of the Yaghan language, which has one remaining native speaker, the author Cristina Calderon. "Your name would be different if I called to you from a canoe, or from the shore; your name would be different if earth or water lay between us." Often, what is untranslatable between two languages is not a word or a phrase but a deeper structuring. Kanien'kéha speaker Chelsea Sunday, for example, notes the following: "Inside of our language, you can't really say anything without relating to something else. You have to relate yourself to things around you."

The untranslatable is inherent in all intercultural contact, where its particles may accumulate and become tropes of otherness. This is dangerous; at the same time, I have trouble believing in an explicatory process by which we become fully known to each other—not only because we remain enigmatic at our hearts, but also because I find it tough to picture a method free from existing hierarchies. It's an old predicament; marginal communities, already fluent for their own survival's sake in the practices of the dominating culture, are asked to do the uphill work of translating themselves to a group that has rarely practiced any decent or imaginative listening.

Rainer Maria Rilke was referring to lovers when he wrote, in that third Germanic tongue: "(…)once the realization is accepted that even between the closest people infinite distances exist, a marvellous living side-by-side can grow up for them, if they succeed in loving the expanse between them, which gives them the possibility of always seeing each other as a whole and before an immense sky." I locate in his words a socio-cultural instructiveness as well; the phrase "if they succeed in loving the expanse between them" is an invitation to respect the untranslatable where it is found; to let go of infusing it with the worst of assumptions; to consider it the sacred foundation of all relations, over which translation's intermittent sparks may astonish us.

yoghurt / yogurt

When my daughter was born, I spoke Dutch to her. It wasn't a deliberate attempt at a bilingual childhood, it was only what happened to me, flooded with such love and devotion and concern and upheaval: murmurings, songs, first namings, even spoken instructions to myself as I groped through the kitchen in an exhausted fog. We had, until then, been an anglophone household, but her father chimed in as much as he could.

When I was out with her, some people asked if I was speaking Arabic. I liked our private tongue. What I was learning to hold in public was not only her small bundled self, but also an enormous, unwieldy affection; it seemed protective that it had its own language.

As a toddler, her favourite stuffie was a monkey named *Aapje*. She fell asleep to a lullaby about a *schaap met witte voetjes*, a sheep with little white feet. It usually took a very long time, and I would stay in bed beside her, growing drowsy as I sang. Sometimes I felt as if a piece of very delayed luggage arrived then from my own immigration, older and more mysterious than anything I had packed: a willow basket, maybe, or a spindle, or a greasy puff of raw wool.

Ideas circled in my tired mind during those months, inconclusive but persistent. I thought of my daughter absorbing my vaginal flora in one astonished birthing gulp. Of the maternal mitochondria that swam in her cells, as they had in a multitude of generations. I pictured my Nani, who ate the earthen balls from the Nairobi market when she was pregnant, and my Oma, fermenting unpasteurized milk for her five children. It felt urgent to make this same yogurt, and I was also sure that it contained strains of organisms so local to *Nederland* that I could never recover them. I heard my friend practice introducing herself in her native Oneida by naming five generations of her foremothers. Among the enigmatic motherly inheritances, language seemed to take its natural place.

Around my daughter's second birthday, there was a shift. She had started to notice that our exchanges involved a currency in which the outside world refused to trade. Her own emerging words turned stubbornly to English, and later in the year, when I was advising her to wear her rain boots, she said, "Stop Dutching me!"

I did, essentially, though part of me wishes that I had approached the matter rather like eating vegetables; this isn't optional, my dear, and you may even come to appreciate it. Instead, we continued to read some favourite Dutch books, and retained a basic vocabulary together, but that was all. Her resistance was not the only reason; it was also the sudden bloom of language in her, so stunning to observe—I wanted to encourage that enthusiastic eruption, with its triumphant stutters of new terms, its stringing together of an awkward but functional grammar, even if English was the medium.

Moreover, her wonder was partly my own. I had never done childhood in English. I didn't know the nursery rhymes and I loved reading them to her, no matter how repetitively, both of us absorbing their lilting cadences and peculiar meanings. There was the rising and then disintegrating rhythm of *Little jumping Joan*. The pleasing decelerations at the end of each stanza in *Bat, bat, come under my hat.* And there were charming, odd rhymes—fellow/pillow, gander/together, sure/moor. Those phrasings and sounds were foreign to the metrically and sonically predictable tongue I was raised in. I had learned English in classrooms, and through the dispensary of the television, but now I could witness the missed stage of play.

In certain verses, I recognized the trails of my own language. It made sense to read "Pussycat, pussycat, what did you there," rather than "what did you *do* there." And I understood that the corn that the miller was grinding could be illustrated as wheat.

Then came other classics, new to me as well. The eerie and lonesome *Goodnight Moon*, the jubilant *Cat in the Hat*, the incantatory *Where the Wild Things Are*. It was a joyful education.

At the same time, because of my own dissolved persistence, I was raising a child who would not know the world of Annie M.G. Schmidt. How could there be a childhood without Puk, the boy who drove a tow truck, and lived on top of an apartment building with his cockroach Zaza? The idea alarmed me enough that I found English translations of her books, and read them to my daughter—but it felt as if I was telling her about the stories, instead of actually transmitting them. Some of their magic held across the gap, however; they are books she returns to on her own.

My daughter holds a linguistic duality that I cannot easily fathom. She knows the items in our living room are only lightly tethered to their names. Does she picture the words *stoel* and chair, two helium balloons, tied to the rounded, yellow wooden backs around the table?

I know it will matter, later; I've heard often enough from first-generation Canadians that they wish they spoke their ancestral languages. So I still raise Dutch as a presence in our house, and encounter the protest of her silence, the smile that acknowledges the tectonic pressing of our wills. But when my mother comes over, and she and I believe that we have furtively conversed in Dutch, my daughter's eyes will gleam with what she's understood.

zwijg

It is possible, in Dutch, to be purposefully mute. In English, a similar meaning may be conveyed adjectivally—to be quiet, or silent—but *zwijg* is a verb, and only the negative of an English verb gets at its essence; to not speak, specifically at a moment when speech might be expected. I come from a place where this is the deed, the positive act, the named gesture.

William of Orange, the founding monarch who initiated the Dutch revolt against the Spanish occupation in the sixteenth century, is also known in the Netherlands as *Willem de Zwijger*. In a common history lesson that may be apocryphal, I was taught that Willem had a crucial encounter with the King of France, who told him of intentions to violently eliminate Protestantism from the French and Spanish territories. Willem *zwoog* so that the King continued to confide in him, allowing Willem to anticipate and defuse his strategies. So it became a term of honour; to *zwijg*, in other words, is a founding Dutch virtue.

There are circumstances under which *zwijgen* is heroic, and others in which it is kind, but I don't believe that the action itself is inherently righteous. Frequently, *zwijgen* implies the presence of a silencing power or coercive force. I've heard the complicity of *zwijgen* in the check-out line behind me while I was accused of shoplifting, and I've heard its protective use by children who couldn't risk speaking of their violent homes. A rigidness encloses our bodies with each withholding, a shutting of the musculature. I think of my Oma's face after she died, and how my mother said it had collapsed into an expression she had never seen before; I wonder if that was a release from the effort of *zwijgen*.

I would rather speak, by which I partly mean write. I'd rather do the uncertain work of telling my parents that I arrived here alone, and also in their grip, that my vowels sounded right but my real tongue was stunned—and hear them out, so that we may gather again around the same table and break *brood*/bread/*roti*. I'd rather write grammatically gawky letters to Dutch friends, and continue in English to search for phrases of marrow and bone.

And I would rather deepen my listening where there is *zwijgen*; below its frozen surface, there is always the water that speaks. When I was a child, winters were colder in the Netherlands than now, and the floodplains of the Rijn froze every year, so that it was possible to skate alongside the river, from town to town, in a vastness of fields and sky. Even the grassy ridges between the pastures wore a layer of ice; you could cleave up one side and speed down the other. I had the kind of curled, wooden skates that tied to my shoes; I carved and flew into that landscape and felt free.

We had a family friend, someone whose kind, calloused hands had tied my skates, and he was very skilled at grafting trees. In his vegetable garden stood the odd, Edenic sight of an apple tree that also bore apricots and plums. Perhaps the minds of linguistic migrants are like that tree; the mother tongue is the apple trunk, with roots that penetrate the earth. And our later languages are branches, feeding through the same roots but setting their own fruit.

Apples spoken by the grainy image of a loved one on a laptop screen; handwritten on a birth certificate; stumbled through at a reunion. Apricots heard in a remote settlement; rising over schoolroom desks; tattooed on a forearm. Plums in a threadbare journal; in a YouTube tutorial; a subtitled movie.

And all of them, harvests of words, in our sleeping and waking dreams.

Works Cited

Permissions were obtained wherever possible.

Alfonso, Lester. *Twelve.* National Film Board of Canada, 2008.

Baldwin, James. Interview with Jordan Elgrably. *The Paris Review.* Issue 91, Spring 1984.

Baraka, Amiri. *Preface to a Twenty Volume Suicide Note.* New York: Totem Press/Corinth Books, 1961.

Belafonte, Harry. *The Versatile Mr. Belafonte.* His Master's Voice Records, 1957.

Berger, John. *About Looking.* New York: Pantheon, 1980.

Bydlowska, Jowita. "Caught between languages." Toronto: *The Globe and Mail.* Dec. 6, 2007.

de Coninck, Herman. *Met een klank van hobo.* Amsterdam: van Oorschot, 1980.

Dunne, Nick. "Kanien'kéha: Recognizing code talkers a part of resuscitating the language." Cornwall: *Standard-Freeholder.* Sep. 11, 2019.

El Khayat, Ghita. cited in *The Amazigh Adventures of Le Petit Prince.* by Louis Werner, in AramcoWorld Nov/Dec 2017.

Fadiman, Anne. *The Spirit Catches You And You Fall Down.* New York: Farrar, Straus and Giroux, 1997.

de Genestet, P.A. *Dichtwerken.* (ed. C.P. Tiele) Amsterdam: Gebroeders Kraay, Amsterdam, 1869.

Gerhardt, Ida. *De Gestorvene.* Amsterdam: Atheneum—Polak & Van Gennep, 2001.

Gerhardt, Ida. *Lucretius. De natuur en haar vormen. Boek I en Boek V, vertaling en verantwoording.* Kampen: J.H. Kok, 1942.

Gerhardt, Ida. *Vijf Vuurstenen.* Amsterdam: Athenaeum-Polak & Van Gennep, 1979.

Gerhardt, Ida. *Zeven maal om de aarde te gaan: a selection of her poems by Gerrit Komrij.* Amsterdam: Atheneum-Polak & Van Gennep, 2001.

Haig-Brown, Celia. *Resistance and Renewal: Surviving the Indian Residential School.* Vancouver: Arsenal Pulp Press, 1988.

Heighton, Steven. *The dead are more visible.* Toronto: Knopf Canada, 2012.

Ibghy, Richard and Marilou Lemmens. *The Golden USB.* Kingston, Agnes Etherington Art Centre. August 26–December 3, 2017.

Idzikowska, Ula. *'Taalachterstand' is een stigmatiserend woord.* Movement (website: www.oneworld.nl/categorie/movement/). November 28, 2018.

Jongbloed (ed. 1888). *Statenvertaling.* Genesis 1: 1-31. www.statenvertaling.net/bijbel/gene/1, 2010.

Kafka, Franz. *Letters to Family, Friends, and Editors.* (translators: Richard and Clara Winston) New York: Schocken Books, 1977.

Lawson, Valeria. *Interview with Pina Bausch.* The Sydney Morning Herald, July 15, 2000.

Lindsay, Vachel. *Going-to-the-Stars.* New York: D. Appleton and Co, 1926.

Lovelace, Robert. *Presentation to the New Farm Project 2010 Fall Gathering.* Harrowsmith, Ontario. November 28, 2010.

McCrum, Robert, William Cran and Robert MacNeil. *The Story of English*. New York: Penguin Books, 1987.

Mish, Frederick C. *Webster's Ninth New Collegiate Dictionary*. Markham, Ontario: Thomas Allen & Son Ld. 1987.

Möhlmann, Thomas (ed.). *Awater*. London: Anvil Press Poetry, 2010.

Nasr, Ramsey. *Mi have een droom*. Amsterdam: de Bezige Bij, 2018.

Nijhoff, Martinus. *Kritisch en verhalend proza (Verzameld werk II)*. (ed. Gerrit Borgers en Gerrit Kamphuis). Amsterdam: Bert Bakker, 1982.

Peerbaye, Soraya. *Poems for the Advisory Committee on Antarctic Names*. Fredericton: Goose Lane Press, 2009.

Rilke, Rainer Maria. *Letters to a Young Poet*. (transl. M.D Herter Norton). London: Norton, 1993.

Singh, Jagjit. *Mirage*. Saregama Records, 1996.

Tippett, Krista. *Mary Oliver: Listening to the World*. On Being. National Public Radio. Feb 5, 2015.

Van der Klis, Hans. "Moeder en Dochter Over Honderd Jaar Verbeelding en Vertaling." *Flaptekst* 7-11-2007. http://flaptekst.blogspot.com/2012/11/moeder-en-dochter-over-100-jaar-astrid.html

Vasalis, M. *De Oude Kustlijn.* Amsterdam: van Oorschot, 2004.

Vasalis, M. *Vergezichten en gezichten.* Amsterdam: van Oorschot, 1954.

Vroman, Leo. 262 Gedichten. Amsterdam: Querido, 1974.

Vroman, Leo. *Uit Slaapwandelen.* Amsterdam: Querido, 1957.

Yildiz, Y. *Beyond the Mother Tongue: The Postmonolingual Condition.* New York: Fordham University Press, 2011.

Acknowledgements

My deep gratitude goes to my family, friends, and
the Villanelles.

Thank you to Don Share, Christian Wiman, and
rob mclennan, whose questions regarding the language in my poems sparked this project.

Previous versions of these essays appeared
in *BRICK magazine, Poetry Magazine, The New
Quarterly, Arc Poetry Magazine*, and *The Poetry
Review*, as well as on *lithub.com*. Many thanks to the
editors and production teams of these publications.

Thank you to C.A. Smid for the cover photograph taken on Texel island.

Thank you to all at Palimpsest Press, and to
Aimée Parent Dunn in particular.

Jim Johnstone was the ideal editor for this project; I am so grateful for his astute and kind work.

I am thankful to the Ontario Arts Council and
the Jean Royce Fellowship for funding this project.

About the Author

Sadiqa de Meijer was born in Amsterdam to a Dutch-Kenyan-Pakistani-Afghani family, and moved to Canada as a child. Her poetry collections are *Leaving Howe Island* (2013) and *The Outer Wards* (2020). Her poetry has received multiple awards, and her first book was a finalist for the Governor General's Literary Award and the Pat Lowther Memorial Award.